Arts and Crafts of
Tamilnadu

LIVING TRADITIONS OF INDIA

Arts and Crafts of
Tamilnadu

Nanditha Krishna
Photographed by V.K. Rajamani

Mapin Publishing Pvt. Ltd., Ahmedabad.

NOTE : The spellings in this book have followed the Tamil alphabet. Unlike Sanskrit which has aspirates, Tamil has none. Thus "t" is pronounced as in temple and "th" as in thimble. Vowels, too, are distinctive. In Tamil "a" is pronounced as a short "a" and "aa" as a long "a". The same rule applies to the other vowels. To standardise the spelling of the Indian words, particularly those in italics, the Tamil phonetic spelling has been followed for Sanskrit words as well, as that is how Sanskrit words would be written in Tamil. Proper nouns, including the names of Gods, people and places, follow the popular Tamil phonetic spelling of words in English, with or without incorporating the above phonetic rules.

Nanditha Krishna

First published in the United States of America in 1992
by Grantha Corporation, 80 Cliffedgeway
Middletown, NJ 07701
in association with
Mapin Publishing Pvt. Ltd.
Chidambaram, Ahmedabad 380 013 India

Text and photographs copyright © 1992 by
Grantha Corporation

ISBN 0-944142-21-4
LC No. 88-82472.

Editorial Consultant : Carmen Kagal
Designer : Dolly Sahiar
Project Facilitation : Quintessence

Typeset in Korina
by Akar Typographics Pvt. Ltd., Ahmedabad.
Printed and bound by
Tien Wah Press (Pte.) Ltd., Singapore

Contents

Introduction

As they approach the Coromandel Coast, the Eastern Ghats turn away, to meet the Western Ghats in the Nilgiris. There are a few hills in the area, but the plain steadily increases in width southwards. This is the Kaveri basin, the heart of Tamilaham, the home of the Tamils, or Tamilnadu, the land of unnumbered temples, of indigenous arts and of almost prehistoric industries. Here, artificial irrigation was practised in the remote past, and some of the most ancient prehistoric settlements of India were located in this area.

The language, Tamil, belongs to the Dravidian group, now found in South India. It has been found to have connections with the languages of the Hurrians of the eastern Euphrates region, the Kassites of southern Iran, the Elamites of Mesopotamia, and Brahui still spoken in Baluchistan. There are cultural affinities with the Elamites, Sumerians, Babylonians and the Indus Valley people. The old theory of the Aryans forcing the non-Aryans to the south has given way to the more probable explanation of the migration of an iron-using megalithic people by sea, an event substantiated by archaeological evidence and literary allusion. The Queen of Sheba and Hiram, King of Tyre, imported items of South Indian origin, including sandalwood and peacocks.

Obviously, then, the South was known to the West at an early period. Pliny and the unknown author of the *Periplus* have written about the towns of the Tamil country between AD 75 and 79, Ptolemy in AD 163. The *Periplus* mentions pepper, pearls, ivory, silk, fine muslin, transparent stones, diamonds, rubies and tortoise-shell as the local produce of Limurike (Tamilaham). The area was also an important re-trading centre for spices and other produce from Malaysia and Indonesia (Jambudvipa).

Records of migration of people from North to South India are lost in the mists of legend. The sage Agasthya is accredited with this move — it is said that he drank the ocean and crossed the Vindhyas. Agasthya is also regarded as the founder-president of the first two Tamil Sangams, or academies of poets and writers. However only the works of the third Sangam are available, a veritable cornucopia of literature. Agasthya is believed to be the author of the first Tamil grammatical treatise, the Agathiyam, which is lost. The stories about him are so many and so diverse that it is impossible to distinguish fact from fiction. However, except for the Agasthya legend, Tamil literary traditions generally speak of the advent of the various Tamil tribes from the sea.

Kautilya refers to the pearls of the Thaamraparni river in the Pandyan country, to cotton fabrics from Madurai, *vaidoorya* (beryl) and sandalwood carvings. Megasthenes mentions the kingdom of Mathura, in the South, ruled by Pandaia, a daughter of Herakles (probably Krishna, as he was known to the Greeks). This has given rise to the belief that the Pandyas are descendants of the Pandavas. Pliny, too, mentions the Pandoe, a race ruled by women, a tradition supported by the *Silappadikaaram* and *Manimekhalai*, the two famous Tamil epics. These refer to Mathurapathi, the queen of Madurai, as the founder of the Pandyan dynasty. Ashoka mentions the kingdoms of the Chola, Pandya and Satiyaputa (of Coimbatore and Salem) in his second edict. Numerous Brahmi inscriptions are found in the South with a script variation of their own, known as Tamil Brahmi. The language is Tamil, except for two from Arikamedu which are in Prakrit. After the Ashoka inscriptions, the only reference to the land of the Tamils is from an inscription of Kharavela of Kalinga in 155 BC, who claimed to have destroyed a confederacy of Tamil states.

Toda woman in her traditional jewellery

No other Tamil community wears silver to the same extent as the Todas.

Following page

The Vivekananda Rock Memorial, Kanyakumari

The Arabian Sea, the Bay of Bengal, and the Indian Ocean merge at the tip of the Indian subcontinent, in Tamilnadu.

TAMILNADU

Scale 1:32 00 000
Kilometers

0   50   100   150   200

State Boundary
District Boundary

KARNATAKA
Bangalore

ANDHRA PRADESH

A

Madras

DHARMAPURI

D

NILGIRIS

N

UDHAGAMANDALAM

TAMILNADU

SALEM

PONDICHERRY

Palar

Ponnaiyar

Vellar

Cauvery

TIRUCHCHIRAPPALLI

PUDUKKOTTAI

I

KERALA

Vaigai

RAMANATHAPURAM

Vaippar

Chittar

INDIA*

Trivandrum

NAGERCOIL

SRI
LANKA

List of places mentioned in the text.

1. Chengalpattu D1
2. Chetinandi C3
3. Chidambaram D2
4. Cuddalore D2
5. Devakottai C3
6. Dharmapuri C2
7. Gingoo D2
8. Gongokondocholapuram D2
9. Kanchipuram D1
10. Kanniyakumari B4
11. Karalkkudi C3
12. Karur C2
13. Kaveripatanam C1
14. Kumbakonam D2
15. Kuttalam B4
16. Madras D1
17. Madurai C3
18. Mamallapuram D1
19. Manamadurai C3
20. Nagappattinam D3
21. Nagore D3
22. Namakkal C2
23. Omalur C2
24. Ooty B2
25. Palani B3
26. Panruti D2
27. Pondicherry D2
28. Ponneri D1
29. Poompuhar D2
30. Papanasam D2
31. Ramanathapuram C4
32. Rameswaram D4
33. Saldapet D1
34. Sankarankovil C4
35. Sivakasi C4
36. Thanjavur D3
37. Tiruchchirappalli C3
38. Tirunelveli C4
39. Tiruvari D3
40. Velanganni D3
41. Vellore D1

But the documentation of the history of the Tamils begins with the Sangam literature, dating to a period between the second century BC and the second century AD consisting of 8 anthologies and 2,279 poems. The land was divided between the Cholas, Cheras and Pandyas and several minor chieftains, most of whom are connected to the Pandavas and Kauravas by the Sangam writers. Simultaneously, there was brisk trade between the Yavanas (Greeks and Romans) and the Tamils, and gold and silver coins of Roman emperors belonging to the first two centuries AD and a Roman settlement at Arikamedu have been important discoveries. The author of the *Periplus* describes the trade between the South and Rome in great detail.

The oldest tribes of the Tamil country were probably the Villavar (or bowmen) and Meenavar (or fishermen). However, the ancient Tamils speak of the Nagas as the ancient rulers of the land and several kings claimed Naga ancestors to legitimise their rule. There is a charming story of the love affair and marriage of the Chola king Killi-Valavan and a Naga princess in the *Manimekhalai*. The later rulers of Tamilaham enlisted Naga warriors in their armies, and tribes such as the Maravar, Eyinar, Oliyar, Oviyar, Aruvalar and Parathavar are referred to as Nagas. Other tribes who ruled the land were the Maarar, Thirayar and Vaanavar, from whom the later Pandyas, Cholas. and Cheras claimed descent.

The third Sangam flourished under the Pandya kings at Madurai. Among the important literary works are the *Tholkaapiyam*, a treatise on grammar; the *Pathupaattu* or ten songs; the *Ettuthohai* or eight anthologies; the *Padinenkizhkanakku* or 18 minor works; the epics of *Silappadikaaram* and *Manimekhalai*; the *Thirukkural*, a code of ethics; and the *Oviyanul*, a treatise on painting. The *Silappadikaaram*, written by the Chera prince Ilango Adigal, is the tragic story of Kannagi and Kovalan, a merchant of the great seaport of Puhar at the mouth of the Kaveri, who leaves his wife for the dancer Madhavi. He spends his fortune on Madhavi and finally returns as a pauper to his faithful wife Kannagi. Kovalan and Kannagi go to Madurai to regain their wealth, where Kovalan is killed, after being falsely accused of stealing the Pandyan queen's anklet. Kannagi proves his innocence, curses the city of

Opposite page

Harvesting

Against a backdrop of stately temples, villagers harvest paddy. Rice is the main crop and agriculture the chief occupation in the state. Every village has a temple with profusely carved *gopurams* (gateways) and *vimaanas* (spires).

Following pages

Gypsy couple

A Nari Kurava (or fox gypsy) couple, unique to Tamilnadu. Wearing a profusion of beads and flowers, they are wanderers who, though feared as thieves, are attractive in their dress and gaiety.

A potter selling her wares under a carved chariot

Past and present, the classical and everyday art, mingle easily in Tamilnadu.

Madurai and dies. *Manimekhalai*, the second epic, written by Cheethalaichaathanar, recounts the story of the daughter of Kovalan and Madhavi who becomes a Buddhist nun. Together, these two epics provide a fascinating glimpse of the lifestyles and traditions of the times. Kannagi is upheld as the ideal of Tamil womanhood, a Tamil Seetha, and is revered and worshipped right up to the present day.

Though many literary references are found, very few architectural monuments remain of the Sangam period. The religion involved an amalgam of Brahminism, village deities, spirit and tree worship, Buddhism and Jainism. As the Sangam age comes to an end, a curtain of darkness is drawn over the history of Tamilnadu for three centuries with the invasion of the Kalabhras, till the sixth century, when the Pallavas of Kanchi and the Pandyas of Madurai rose to prominence.

The state was now divided into four parts Thondaimandalam, consisting of the northern the part which was ruled by the Pallavas; Cholamandalam, the rice belt between Thiruchirapalli (Trichinopoly) and the Kaveri delta which was ruled by the Cholas; Pandiamandalam, the land of the Pandyas, extending to the tip of the peninsula with its capital at Madurai; and Kongu-Cheramandalam, the western part of the state around Coimbatore and Dharmapuri, adjoining Kerala, and ruled by the Chera kings.

The earliest monuments in stone belong to the Pallava period AD 550 to 912. Of these, caves, *rathas* or chariots, and sculptures of Mamallapuram (Mahabalipuram) and Kanchipuram are outstanding. The Pallavas inscribed their epigraphs in Sanskrit and were great patrons of Vaishnavism and Shaivism which fast replaced Buddhism and Jainism, the popular religions earlier. The *bhakthi* movement, which originated in Tamilaham, was a mass cultural development transcending all barriers of caste and it developed from the simple hymns of folk singers to Shiva and Vishnu. Thus the religious outpourings of the saints—the Shaivite Naayanmaars and Vaishnavite Aalwaars—form the backbone of the later Hinduism of Tamilnadu, derived as they were from both Vedic and folk beliefs.

Road–side shrines

Worship of *naagakal* (snake stones) and Ganesha under an *arasamaram* (*pipal* tree). Religion in Tamilnadu involves the worship of the primitive and the sophisticated, with tribal practices mingling with the highest philosophy. The *deepam* (light), *kurnkum, (ver milion) manjal* (turmeric), *kolam* (rice flour designs) and flowers are essential to any ritual.

Simultaneously, the Pandyas ruled from AD 590 to 920 and left cave temples around Thiruchirapalli and Namakkal. They are best known for the paintings in the Jain caves of Sittannavasal in Pudukottai district.

But the classical age of Tamil culture belongs to the period of the Cholas, who ruled from AD 850 to 1279. The *bhakti* movement was now very powerful and Shaivism received official patronage. The great temples of Brihadeeshvara at Thanjavur (Tanjore) and Gangaikondacholapuram, and the temples at Thiruvakkarai, Darasuram and Thribhuvanam, to name a few, are all dedicated to Shiva. The famous bronzes of Tamilnadu reached a stage of perfection and the greatest Natarajas appeared at this time. The other arts, including dance, music, theatre and literature, attained their zenith. The Cholas under Rajaraja I and his son Rajendra I annexed Sri Lanka, Malaya, Orissa (Kalinga) and Bengal, giving Rajendra the title of Gangaikondachola (the Chola who conquered the Ganga). Trade with Southeast Asia, already established by the Pallavas, developed into diplomatic relations and

Tamil culture spread far. Several *nagarams* or urban conglomerations were established by the Cholas, and the Nagarathaars or urban merchants were important conveyors of culture between Tamilaham and the East.

The frequent wars with the Pandyas weakened the Chola kingdoms, and the Pandyas came back to power from AD 1187 to 1308. An important visitor at the Pandya court in Madurai was Marco Polo, who describes the kingdom's great wealth of jewels and pearls and gives a detailed account of trade conditions and social customs prevailing at the time.

After a short period (AD 1365 to 1370) as a sultanate, Madurai was taken over in AD 1370 by the Vijayanagara kings, who consolidated their supremacy all over Tamilnadu. This was a period of frenzied artistic activity. The seeds were sown for the heavy stylisation of the various art forms and much of today's art is derived from the love of the baroque developed during this period. After the terrible battle of Talikota in 1564 and the rout of the Vijayanagara army, Tamilnadu was carved up by local chieftains. The most important of these were the Nayaks, of whom Thirumala Nayak was a great patron of the arts. The various city-states were engaged in wars with each other, supporting the survivors of the Vijayanagara empire, and frequently changed hands, going from local chieftains to the Marathas and the Muslims, till they all finally fell to the British. After the Nayaks, the arts had little or no patronage and their rapid degeneration set in.

Through all these turbulent political upheavals, religion remained a major motivating force in Tamilnadu. The temple was the centre of authority, the focus of all activity, with the shops and houses planned around it. There can be no village without at least one temple — in fact, a village without a temple is likened to a man without a soul. The religion varies from the primitive worship of Kali, Mariamman and *bhootas* (spirits), accompanied by blood sacrifice, liquor and-magic, to the most sophisticated forms of Hinduism. In fact, the role of religion is so important that most crafts have been adapted to serve religious needs — from the bronzes depicting the gods to simple basketry, where even the designs and weave may have cosmic connotations. The local adaptations of Hindu deities became popu-

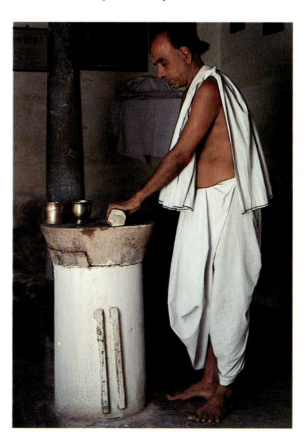

Daily prayers

A priest grinding sandalwood for his daily prayers. Ritual plays an important part in daily life and each family has its own rituals which are handed down through generations.

lar cult figures, so that Karthikeya is better known as Murugan with his two wives, Vishnu as Ranganatha, Krishna as Venugopala, and Shiva as Nataraja, the lord of dance. The deep, strong roots of religion have provided a binding force and a permanence for Tamil culture, ensuring a continuity of tradition and a major role for the arts.

Because classical culture has always been strong and religion deep-rooted, the folk crafts became classicised—the village terracottas became the great bronzes, the wood carvings became great monuments in stone. Thus, it is very difficult to tell an art form apart from a craft. The basic insularity of the culture protected it from extraneous influences which could have changed its form, as happened elsewhere in India. Instead, the creative genius of the people and their love for the fine arts strengthened the styles from within. Indeed, it may even be said that stylisation and regression of art in Tamilnadu commenced only after the introduction of outside elements during the Vijayanagara period.

Although the whole state shares a common language and culture, various parts developed their own distinct styles. If the metalware and woodwork of Chettinad are notable for their design, the work in Thondaimandalam, the area surrounding Kanchipuram, is known for its unique shape and elegant simplicity. Textiles have their own local variations in weave and colour, yet the tradition of contrasting borders is common everywhere.

Away from the mainstream of Tamil life are the tribes who have their own distinctive cultures. The most notable of these are the Todas of the Nilgiris, whose origins are shrouded in speculation. The Badagas and Kotas of the Nilgiris, the Kadars of the Aanamalai and the Maravars of the plains are among many who were slowly-absorbed into Hindu society, and yet retained several of their traditions. The gypsies, too, are unique in Tamilnadu. They are known as Nari Kuravas (fox gypsies, from their habit of fox hunting) and dress differently from the neighbouring Lambadis of Andhra Pradesh. The Nari Kurava women wear short skirts and a short blouse, the men the smallest of *dhotis*. Covered with a profusion of colourful beads, they are objects of both fear and fascination wherever they go.

The post-independence period in Tamilnadu has seen a considerable effort to revive several languishing crafts and today handicrafts have become a big industry. They are major items of export, sent to markets abroad as well as all over the country. The sophistication of these crafts has made it possible for them to be adapted easily to contemporary requirements. Yet, this has not necessarily been beneficial, and indiscriminarte commercialisation has in many cases marred the beauty of the old craft forms.

But some traditions die hard in India, particularly in Tamilnadu, and the ritual *kolam*, done with great reverence and creativity outside her door by the ordinary housewife, is still a work of beauty. Terracotta horses are still placed as votive offerings in temples; traditional textiles and jewellery are still worn at every festival and wedding; and a bride's trousseau must still include her prayer items. The strong role played by religion, with which most crafts are closely inter-linked has ensured the preservation of tradition and beauty in the traditional Tamil home.

Opposite page

Mamallapuram

The shore temples of Mamallapuram, the site of the beginnings of stone carving in Tamilnadu. The art later reached great heights in the history of India.

India, the home of cotton, was a major textile centre from very early times. In the Old Testament, Job's patience and wisdom are compared to the fastness of Indian dyes. As far back as 2000 BC, the Roman word for cotton, *carbasina* was derived from the Sanskrit *karpasa*. A Roman emperor decried the vanity of women who craved for Indian muslin, saying that it emptied the emperor's coffers of gold. In Nero's time, "Indian muslins were known as nebula venti or woven winds".

The dry hot climate of Tamilnadu has been the home of luminous silks and brightly-hued cottons. The colours are woven together — one for the border and *pallu* and another for the body, creating a rich effect by their colour contrasts and tonal blending. This tradition of combining the most unlikely colours has produced startlingly attractive results.

The earliest records speak of the fine muslins and silks from Tamilnadu. In the *Periplus of the Erythrean Sea*, it is said that Greek traders came to Uraiyur, a great centre of cotton trade, to buy fine cloth and silks, particularly hand-painted or printed calicoes. The author mentions cotton cloth, as thin as the slough of a snake or a cloud of steam, so finely woven that the eye could not follow the course of the thread. From the seventh to third centuries BC, Bengal and Orissa, Varanasi (Benares) and Madurai were famous for silk and cotton weaving. Kautilya notes that Madurai produced the finest cotton fabrics, and the *Mahabharatha* also mentions the textiles of the Tamil kingdom. Thanjavur produced a muslin called *agartic*. Among the gifts presented at the coronation of Yudhishthira were pure muslins from this region.

During the Sangam age, silk and cotton weaving reached a high degree of perfection. The Sangam writers tell us that spinning was the part-time-occupation of women, a tradition that continues till today. The *Porunarrupadai* refers to silk cloth with its threads knotted at the ends. The *Silappadikaaram* abounds in references to textiles. It mentions the weavers, known as Karukas, of Kaveripattinam, who spun silk, cotton and wool to be later stitched by tailors for women to wear. There were streets in Puhar reserved only for fine fabrics.

Madhavi, the dancer in the story, is described wearing a blue cloth embroidered with flowers, from which we gather that embroidery was also practised. The girls were fond of multicoloured clothes, says the epic, and had different clothes for the day and for the night. The Eyinar tribe is described as dressing their goddess in the tiger skins and elephant skins worn by them. There is a reference to Madurai which had a special street for cloth merchants whose shops were piled high with bales of cloth.

Sangam literature says that whereas poor people wore only one garment, the rich wore two, including an upper garment, hung over the shoulder. Cotton could be either coarse or fine, the finer-variety compared to the vapour of milk. Floral designs were most popular on the silks, which could be washed and laundered. This tradition of producing strong silks which can be laundered continues till today. Spinning, says Sangam literature, was a major occupation of widows.

Each caste had its own colour predilictions. Brahmins decked their deities in white silk, Kshatriyas in red silk, Vaishyas in yellow silk and Vellalas in bright *kalakam* (mixture). Most married women wore yellow *alkuls* or lower garments. The *Manimekhalai* speaks of the artistic patterns of the cloth and the dexterity of the weavers.

Carpet weaving

This photograph depicts a Jambai carpet in the process of being woven. The cotton *jamakaalam* durrie is brightly coloured. The yarn is coarse, and the weft is of a striped design. The durrie is used for lying on or as a mat to sit on during a meal.

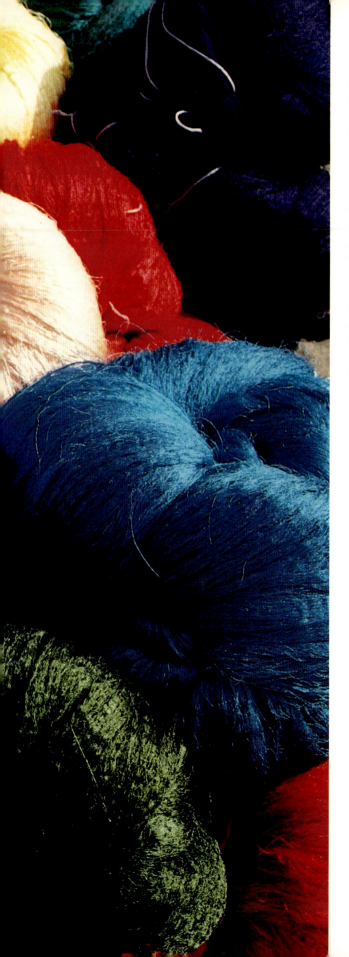

In the second millenium there was a flourishing trade between Tamilnadu and China, and silks were exchanged between the two. Thus the word *sinam* (meaning that which came from China) was occasionally used for silk. This has led several historians to wonder whether silks could have been of Chinese origin. The later Tamil word for silk, *pattu*, actually means a fold, from the cotton cloth folded and hung over the shoulder. Among the goods exported were satin and cotton cloth, *karpasa* to the Hebrews; vegetable–dyed cloth to Assyria; and lace and dyed cottons to Persia. Ctesias, a Greek who worked at the court of Darius II in the fifth century BC records that the Persians received fabrics dyed with a colour obtained from red beetles. Silk reached the faraway Mediterranean coast through the empires of Darius and Xerxes, and a kind of gauze reached Tyre. The edict of the Roman emperor Diocletian mentions stuffed mattresses and pillows made from Indian cotton. There appears to have been some confusion among the Greeks and Romans regarding Indian cotton and silk, for they described both as "tree-wool".

The importance of the textile trade can be gauged from the fact that the Chola capital Uraiyur, the Chera capital Karur and the Pandya capital Madurai were situated in the vicinity of cotton-growing areas. Cotton was brought to these capitals to be woven and the flourishing trade that ensued enabled them to attain the privilege of becoming the state's capitals. These towns continue to be prosperous centres of cotton textiles even today.

Later visitors have made several references to the textiles of Tamilnadu. Chau-ju-kua, a Chinese traveller of the 13th century, says that the Cholas, especially the princes, wore only cotton clothing, as that was the prevailing custom. The 16th century Portuguese traveller Fernao Nuniz mentions the quilted cotton tunics of the Chola soldiers, while another traveller observes that the people in the Pandya country wore a short cotton skirt (probably the folded *dhoti* or *veshti*, the lower garment), and a cloth of gold and silk over their heads. The king wore a quilted cotton robe and a garment of gold piastres over it.

According to Marco Polo, who visited the Pandyan kingdom in the 15th century, ships used

Opposite page

The colours of Tamilnadu

The wide range of colours used for Kanchipuram silk sarees is vividly shown in these bundles.

(Courtesy : Weavers Service Centre, Kanchipuram)

Following pages

Toda women outside their hut embroidering their shawls

The Todas are a fast-dwindling tribe living in the cool hills of the Nilgiris. They retain their own customs and manner of living. The cold climate requires the use of shawls by both men and women.

Cotton saree, Kanchipuram

Kanchipuram cotton saree with a *rudraaksham* and *vanki* design on the border. The *rudraaksham* is a sacred nut and the *vanki* is the armlet worn over the *choli*. The designs on Kanchipuram cotton sarees are given a relief effect by the use of the Jacquard weave.

Centre

Silk saree with a striped body and a lotus motif both in the border and the *pallu*.

(Courtesy : Charu Rajamani)

Cotton saree, Kanchipuram

(See p. 25)

Right

Kanchipuram shot-silk saree with a *mayil–kazhuthu* (peacock-neck) coloured body, and a shocking pink border and *pallu*

The body colour is formed by alternating deep blue and green threads in the warp and weft.

(Courtesy : Nanditha Krishna)

silk and gold cloth as ballast while sailing from the Pandyan kingdom to the kingdom of Eli (Mount d'Ely). He was amazed at the scantiness of clothing and has denied the existence of tailors, although earlier literary and inscriptional-evidence points to the contrary. The Portuguese traveller Barbosa notes that, in the 16th century, large quantities of printed cotton were exported to Siam and Burma from Paleacate (Pulicat) on the Coromandel Coast. Paes, a Portuguese traveller, goes into raptures over the rich clothes worn by the women of Raghunatha Nayak's court in Thanjavur. According to Nicholas Pimenta, who visited the Jesuits in India in the 16th century, the Nayak of Gingee always wore silk and presented him with gold-wrought clothes.

Service to the king or state was recognised by the award of a cloth with a title inscribed on it. In AD 1004, the Chola king Rajakesarivarman Perumanadigal granted the privilege of wearing an inscribed silk cloth to one Manija. Weavers were generally held in high esteem, but those of Kanchipuram alone had the right to use the *sangu* (conch) and *dandu* (palanquin).

As with all other crafts in India, weaving and dyeing are hereditary occupations. Interestingly, many weavers in Tamilnadu are of Telugu origin. The important weaving communities include the Sengundam Mudaliar. Pattunoolkaras. some Komatis, Kaikolar, Seniyar, Saliyar, Devangar, Salava, Padma-Sale and Pattu-Sale. The older printing areas were around Ponneri, Arcot, Pudukottai, Saidapet, Kumbakonam, Thanjavur and Nagapattinam.

Before Kanchipuram became known for silk weaving, Kumbakonam and its surrounding-areas were regarded as the traditional silk weaving centres. Kanchipuram has since practically become synonymous with silk weaving and the silk saree of Tamilnadu is often referred to as a Kanchi silk. The uniqueness of a Kanchipuram silk saree is that the border and *pallu* are woven separately and then attached to the body of the saree. Generally, the design in the border is repeated across the *pallu*. We find patterns of the swan, parrot, peacock or elephant depicted along with creeper-like backgrounds. These forms were adopted from South Indian temple architecture and sculpture. The rich Kanchi silks are some-

times known as temple sarees, from the practice of gifting them to temple deities.

The art of silk weaving already existing around Kumbakonam was reinforced by Bengali traditions when Tippu Sultan sent an emissary to learn the trade. This resulted in the blouse materials of Ariyalur and Ayyampettai.

The quality of silk in Tamilnadu is excellent. For example, Kanchipuram silks are washed, even beaten on a granite stone, and have survived several generations. The body may be plain, striped, checked or covered with delicate buds known as *mallimoggu* (jasmine buds). Thanjavur specialises in weaving brocade sarees covered all over with *zari* (gold thread) and used for weddings and in temples. The borders of these sarees are rich and broad, heavy with gold, and the *pallu* is covered with designs from temple friezes. The *yaali* (mythical lion) and *hamsa* (mythical bird) continue to be common motifs. In addition to Kanchipuram, Kumbakonam and Thanjavur are important centres of silk weaving. Arni produces a light-weight variety of silk woven with a fly shuttle. Here, the *pallu* is a continuation of the saree warp and the border design is in *zari*. Arni silks are woven in checks outlined in gold and black, with the meshes of the checks in orange or red. A popular product is "shot silk", where two different colours combine in the body to produce different shades according to the play of light.

The Thanjavur weavers formerly had a special weaving technique which is now lost. The designs were created with gold thread let into the weft, which formed the background. The saree was then waxed and certain areas dyed to produce a shaded effect. The process of dyeing toned down the brightness of the gold. Single weft or warp (*ikat*) silks and cotton were to be found in Kumbakonam, Thanjavur and Thiruchirapalli, but are no longer produced.

In Tamilnadu, the cotton sarees follow the pattern of woven silk very closely. Cotton weaving is still very widespread—in Kanchipuram, Salem, Pudukottai, Madurai, Shankaramkovil, Uraiyur, Karur and Coimbatore.

The heavy cotton *dungari* from Kanchipuram was the origin of the later British dungarees.

Opposite page

Kalamkari, Sickinaikenpet

The village of Sickinaikenpet in Thanjavur district is the only place where this art is practised in Tamilnadu, and is restricted to the members of one single family. The colours used here are much brighter than their counterparts elsewhere. While the art had become very lack-lustre, there has been a great effort at design development in recent years.

Coimbatore sarees are famous for their decorative floral borders. Uraiyur in Thiruchirapalli district, and Salem are noted for their fine count cotton sarees, although the latter is better known for men's *veshtis*, both silk and cotton. The *kuyil-kan* (cuckoo's eye) and *mayil-kan* (peacock's eye) border in three-shuttle weave is the exclusive monopoly of Salem weavers. The cottons of Madurai, particularly the white *veshtis*, either plain or with a *zari* or coloured border, are favoured for their sturdy weave and fine quality.

But Madurai is better known for its *chungidi* and *thombu* sarees. Made by a community known as the Saurashtras, who originally migrated from Gujarat, they are tie-dyed, with a contrasting border containing the traditional *rudraaksham* or sovereign design, and a *pallu* with a paisley design in the corner, in *jaamdani* style.

The most indigenous or local elements are best seen in the Chettinad fabrics. Unlike the usual saree width of about 120 cm, these sarees have a width of only about 91.5 cm. They were originally produced in Karaikudi and are dyed in earthy hues such as mustard, brick red, and black. Locally known as *kandaangi selai*, these sarees

are worn at calf-length, thus enabling the woman to display her silver anklets.

Cotton and silk mixtures, such as the Kurainaadu and Kodambakkam sarees, may have a cotton body and a mixed silk and cotton border, or may be mixed throughout. In the past, *naar pattu*, or banana fibre, used to be yet another popular material for weaving, but this is practically extinct today.

The most common construction of a saree consists of borders on each side and a broad *pallu*. Decoration is largely geometric and includes the *rudraaksham, uthiri poo* (loose flowers), *mopla-petu* (Moplah design), *chalangai* (bells), *vanki* (armlet), *panirchombu* (rose-water pot), *metti* (toe ring) and many more designs. These are combined with stylised motifs of mangoes, lotuses, birds and animals. Other popular designs weaving the border into the body include *veld-haari* (horizontal wavy lines), *vaazhai poo (*banana flower), *thaazhambu* (screw pine flower), *muthuchir, oosivaanam* (literally, the needle sky) and *pancharangi* (five colours). A wide range of checks includes *kottadi, paalayankottai, muthu-kandi, paaimadi,* and *papli,* indicating their size and construction. The *pallu* may be elaborate, with a variety of birds, animals, flowers and geometric designs, or simple, carrying over the border colour and design.

In the 18th century there was a booming *kalam-kari* (pen painting) trade between India and Europe. The designs were known as *cheeti* in Tamil, from which it is said the European chintz is derived. In 1734, Monsieur de Beaulieu, a French naval officer, wrote a detailed account of the *kal-am* work and the dyeing process as practised in Pondicherry. Coimbatore was famous for its hand-painted *cheeti* over a white or gray background. The designs were bold, in free-hand and consisted of birds, animals, flowers and creepers. The borders were wide and decorated, with contrasting colours. Painted in blue, the designs could be seen on both sides of the material's dark red background. The most popular vegetable dyes were rich reds, black, yellow and the native indigo. Though chemical dyes are increasingly used today, the art of *kalamkari* still retains the use of vegetable dyes.

Block printing in Pudukottai, known for its fine wax-resist printing.

By this method the motifs were first printed on the cloth with wax and then dyed. After this, the wax was removed. This is similar to the process of pen-batik.

(Courtesy : Weavers Service Centre, Madras)

Kalamkari artist R. Emperumal at work

This art is restricted to Sickinaikenpet in Thanjavur District. It is hand-painted, using a stick wound with thread and dipped in dye. The artist belongs to a long line of *kalamkari* artists who came into Tamilnadu from Andhra Pradesh.

Winding the yarn for the warp

Spinning and winding are done by the women, while the men weave the material.

Bottom

Tie-dye, Madurai

This picture demonstrates the Madurai *chungidi* tie and dye process. The woman is shown tying the material for the dyeing of the next colour. The weavers are of Saurashtra origin, and the process was obviously imported from Gujarat. However, it has been adapted to include the Tamil tradition of contrasting borders, as the lady's saree indicates.

Cotton carpet

A Bhavani cotton carpet (*jamakaalam*) with designs on all four sides and a decorative motif in the centre.

The designs which evolved during the Nayak period continue today, albeit with an element of distortion. The wall hangings of the Nayak period depict processions and religious themes with highly stylised figures. The design forms in vogue until the early part of the 17th century are depicted in the costumes of the figures, with enchanting geometrical patterns in the background echoing a suggestion of architectural concepts.

The Karupoor saree, which evolved under the patronage of the Maratha rulers, has a unique place among textiles. A combination of intricate weave and wax-resist hand-painted designs, was used exclusively for royal weddings. In the *pallu*, the design motifs are woven in cotton (*jaamdani* weave) and the border with *zari* weft. This combination of cotton and *zari* in the *jaamdani* weaving technique was done in order to leave room for hand-painting. The *zari* woven in patterns shines through the hand-painted areas and the combination produces an effect at once rich and delicate. The body gold is in *ashrafi* (coin) design, whereas the *pallu* and border have intricate gold trees. Red was the base, and the outline was executed in black.

To the same variety of sarees belong the hand-painted and wax-resist fabrics from Pudukottai, examples of which can be seen in the local museum. The wax-resist printing used perforated brass plate blocks and care was taken not to make the wax hot, in which case it would penetrate the fabric completely. This method is totally lost today.

The tradition of *kalamkari* is carried on by a single family at Sickinaikenpet in Thanjavur district. The wall hangings, door frames and *thombais* (tubular hangings) have epic and Puraanic themes and are hand-painted in vegetable colours. However, the stylisation of the figures has deviated greatly from tradition.

In Thanjavur and Kumbakonam, cotton appliqué decorates the *rathas* or chariots used for the temple festival. It is a kind of collage, made of felt and cotton in rich, bright colours.

The Madras handkerchief, also known as "Bleeding Madras" because of the indigo dye which runs, was popular for its bold colours and checks. Today, fast colours are used in its production.

Salem is the home of the Bhavani durrie, woven in silk and cotton in brilliant colours. The lotus decorates the centre, and the border has either flowing floral patterns or stylised parrots.

The craft of lace-making was introduced into Tamilnadu by Portuguese and Dutch missionaries. The lace-making industry of the state is generally acknowledged as the finest in the country, with a variety of cotton and silk lace, some including gold and silver thread.

Jaali or net embroidery has also been popular and, though resembling drawn-thread work, is actually achieved by forcing the warp and weft threads apart with a needle and fixing them in position with minute button-hole stitches. Embroidery was introduced by the Muslims who have left their imprint on the designs, the geometrical and floral shapes.

The textiles of Tamilnadu are among the richest in the country. Many traditions have continued unchanged over the centuries and the quality of the silks has ensured that several examples remain of the creations of the past. However, it is also true that many traditions have been lost and have been impossible to reproduce in spite of the tremendous effort made in the last few years. The

Young girl's skirt and blouse

A girl's *paavaadai* and *chokkaai* or skirt and blouse made of silk, depicting animal and mango motifs.

(Courtesy : Nanditha Krishna)

Opposite page

Wedding Saree

This is the *pallu* of an original Kodali-Karupoor saree. The wedding saree of the Maratha rulers of Tanjore, these sarees were of cotton, with a combination of weaving, hand-painting and *zari* (gold brocade) work. They were found in the village of Karupoor.

(Courtesy : College of Arts & Crafts, Madras)

Weavers' Service Centre in Madras has contributed greatly to the textile renaissance, reviving some of the glorious designs and weaves of bygone years.

The most famous of Tamilnadu's art forms is probably its bronzes. Over the centuries, they have reached aesthetic heights which place them among the greatest achievements of Indian art. A rare combination of beauty and power has culminated in a sophistication and unique sensitivity, further emphasised by variety and range. The art has continued uninterrupted till today, although the 20th century bronzes continue to be copies of the Pallava and Chola figures and have yet to develop an identity of their own.

These metal images were born out of the community's need to connect the sanctity of the temple with the secular town around it. The main figure in the temple is generally of stone and occasionally of wood, stucco or other materials. Once consecrated, the sthirabera ,or stationary image, could never be moved. Only the chalabera , uthsavamurthi or moving images could be taken out of the temple. These, said the Aagamas (canons of art), had to be made out of metal.

The festival is known as uthsavam or thiruvizhaa. The nithyothsavams are daily festivals and the mahothsavams are annual or "great" festivals. The daily procession of the deity around the village is an important event, eagerly awaited as part of the morning routine. In Vishnu temples, the uthsavamurthis are known as kautukabera. Metal images of the same form as the consecrated deity are placed in front of it and receive regular worship; in fact, the daily ritual is considered incomplete without them. The main deities are taken out in procession only during the annual festivals.

The Sangam literature of the beginning of the Christian era speaks of the daily procession of deities led by Lord Shiva and the evening festival (anthivilaa) both of Madurai. In the seventh century, Shaivite saints sang with reverence of the

processional images. Inscriptions and literature refer to the jewellery adorning these deities, the flower garlands, music and dance—taken together, all these constituted an experience to savour. Tamilnadu is fortunate in that the uthsavams or thiruvizhaas are still celebrated with the same fervour and elaboration, thereby continuing the link with a colourful past.

One of the strongest of these links is preserved in the art of bronze casting which still is strictly governed by the canons of iconography and iconometry. The chief canons include the Maulisuthra, Naabhisuthra, Akshisuthra, Bhumisuthra, Kakshasuthra, Maanasara and Shilparathna. The measurement for a bronze figure is the thaala, the distance from the forehead the chin. The figure is prepared according to the cire perdue or lost-wax method, know as the madhuchchhistavidhana. The sthapathis or sculptors were, and continue to be, well-versed in Sanskrit as well as Tamil, both of which are necessary for the study of the Shilpa Shaastras (canons of sculpture). Like all artisans in India, their knowledge and profession are hereditary.

The image is first moulded in wax, then coated with clay strengthened with ground cotton, salt and charred husk. This coating is applied three times. Then the chosen metal is heated and poured into the mould, from which the wax had been heated and removed earlier. The mould is allowed to cool, carefully broken, and the image is brought out. The final touches are given by hand—the finishing, burnishing and perfecting of the minutest details. The figures are generally solid, although less important ones such as Nandi may occasionally be hollow.

The earliest metal objects come from a burial urn found at Adichanallur (circa 500 BC) on the banks of the river Thaamraparni. Thus the tradition of metal sculpture obviously has an ancient

Bronze image of Shanmugha, the six-headed form of Lord Karthikeya

The craftsman gives the final touches to an icon with a chisel and a hammer. Although bronzes are cast in the cire perdue method the finishing touches are given by hand.

past and several historians even trace it as far back as the Harappan period.

The ornamentation, dress, and even the method of moulding have changed through the ages, enabling us to date the figure. There is an inexplicable blank between the Adichanallur metalwork and the Pallava bronzes of the eighth century AD although there are literary references to metal sculpture in this period. The Pallava figures are characterised by their elegant simplicity. As in the case of stone sculpture, the figures have broad, straight shoulders and wear heavy lower garments with a thickly rolled waist-cloth falling between the legs. The *poonal* (sacred thread) resembles a thick strap. The features are also thick-set and heavy. The Pallava bronzes suggest that the minutest details were carved in the wax mould, leaving very little chiselling to be done after the image had been cast.

But the greatest bronzes of Tamilnadu belong to the period of the Cholas, commencing in the 10th century AD. The wax model was, in contrast to the earlier Pallava one, quite rough, and the final chiselling assumed greater importance. From inscriptions, we know that copper was the primary metal and that the bronze images of the Chola period were known merely as *seppu thirumeni* (metal image). Later on, the *panchaloha* or five metals, (copper, tin, lead, silver and gold) became more popular, representing the five elements earth, air, ether, water and fire. Whereas the earlier images were of a copper–brass colour, the later ones have a different hue, suggesting more metals in the alloy.

The three great Cholas who were actively associated with the development of bronzes were Adithya I, Sembiyan Mahadevi and Rajaraja I. Adithya (AD 875-906) claimed to have built 108 temples along the river Kaveri, and some beautiful bronzes were created in his period. The great bronze Natarajas had appeared by the 10th century, during the reign of Paranthaka I (AD 907-955). Sembiyan Mahadevi, his successor, was a Chola queen of exquisite taste who commissioned several bronzes notable for their delicacy. But the greatest belong to the period of Rajaraja I, the builder of the Brihadeeshvara temple at Thanjavur. The Chola style of bronzes continued till the overthrow of the dynasty in the 13th centu-

Opposite page

Nataraja, Lord of Dance

Bronze image of Ganesha, the elephant headed deity

Ardhanarishvara, Thiruvengadu, Thanjavur district, 11th century AD

As the name itself indicates, this is a half-male and half female form, signifying the divine union of Shiva and Shakthi and typifying the male and female energies. The right half represents Shiva and the left, Parvati. The sexual difference between the right half and the left half is meticulously maintained, starting with the head-dress and ending with the foot. Thus, the right half is shown with an axe in the upper arm, and the lower arm is shown as resting on his vehicle. On the left side, the arm is shown in the posture of holding a mirror. The striking features of this piece are the moulding of the torso, the successful balance in proportioning the male and the female sides, and the elegant posture of the respective halves. It is the finest representation of this form in metal. Historically, the image is an important one since there is an inscriptional reference to it in the temple at Thiruvengadu.

(Courtesy : Madras Museum)

Opposite page

Folk deity

Karumariamman, the goddess at Thiruverkadu, a folk deity whose worship has become very popular in recent times. This image is an example of how non-canonical forms are adapted to suit *Shaastraic* requirements of sculpture, and absorbed by the mainstream of Hinduism.

(Courtesy : Poompuhar)

ry and under the Pandyas for another 100 years. However, a decline soon set in and the bronzes of the succeeding Vijayanagara and Nayak dynasties are stiff, stylised and baroque. The aesthetic value was lost in a new-found love of details and embellishment.

The male figures of the Chola period are broad–shouldered and slim-waisted, majestic, supple and calm. The female figures, of Parvathi in particular, are delicate and bashful. There is a very definite suggestion of the strong male protecting the weaker female. If Shiva's legs are muscular and strong, Parvati's are slim and graceful. Drapery is kept to a minimum, and delicately moulded around each limb. The jewels consist of miniaturised pearls and gems, with a small halo or *shiraschakra* at the back. The simplicity of adornment, coupled with the graceful body movements and beautiful expressions raise the Chola bronzes to the level of great art.

Of these, the outstanding figure is of Nataraja, Shiva as the Lord of Dance who creates as he destroys, whose *aananda thaandava* (dance of joy) represents knowledge, happiness and the destruction of evil. The figure suggests vigorous movement within the *prabhaamandala* (the halo of fire) representing the cosmos, yet the precise balancing of the *thaandava* pose and the decorative details suggest an innate calm. The various moods are reflected in the face — joy, serenity and dignity.

Shiva, Parvati and the Naayanmaars, or Shaivite saints, form the majority and the best of the bronzes, due to the predominant Shaivism of the Chola period.

In the past there were about a dozen important bronze casting centres in Tamilnadu. Of these, Kumbakonam alone survives as a major producer of bronzes and the art is concentrated in the village of Swamimalai. A few units may be found on the outskirts of Cuddalore and Thanjavur. The profession is still hereditary and the art a closely-guarded secret.

Due to several centuries of neglect under the British, the bronze industry did not develop a 20th century idiom. The fillip given in the post-independence period has been restricted to cop-

Mother and child, folk bronze, about 18th century

Images such as these were very popular at one time and could have been votive offerings by childless women.

(Courtesy : Aparna Art Gallery)

Top

Working with moulds

The various stages of the mould before the bronze is removed. From left to right : (1) The incomplete bronze image, which must now be finished by hand with a chisel. (2) The broken mould containing the hardened bronze image. (3) The covered mould with the molten bronze inside. (4) The mould with the hole at one end into which the molten bronze is poured. The clay cocoon-like mould is bound with wire.

Image of a mouse

Opposite page

Thirugnanasambandhar, Muhandanur, Thanjavur District, 12th century AD

He is one of the Naayanmaars, the sixty–three saints of Tamil Shaivism. The story goes that his father, the priest at the Sirgazhi temple (Thanjavur district) forgetfully locked the child inside the sanctum sanctorum one night. When he came back the next morning the child was safe, having been fed milk by Parvati. The icon is of the young boy holding a cup of milk in his right hand, with the left hand in the *vismaya mudra,* expressing delight at receiving the divine milk.

(Courtesy : Madras Museum)

Folk bronze of horse and rider.

Probably Ayyanar, a deified hero.

Courtesy : Aparna Art Gallery

Carved lamp

Paavai-vilakku or *deepalakshmi* consists of a female figure carrying a shallow bowl as the light container. The figure is intricately carved and the details of dress, ornaments and hair braid are beautifully fashioned.

(Courtesy : Jagannatha S. Sthapathi, Kumbakonam).

Gajasamharamurthi

Contemporary bronze image of Shiva as the killer of the elephant demon Gajasura

ies of Chola and Pallava figures. These are excellent and many craftsmen have even managed to capture the joyous abandon of the *aananda thaandava* in the figure of a Nataraja or a Gajasamhaaramurti (Shiva destroying the elephant demon). But the figures are still copies, and the craftsmen have yet to create a Nataraja of this century. The depiction of Ganesha has made considerable strides in the last few years, probably due to the contemporary popularity of the god. Ganesha dancing, sitting, standing, even resting, Heramba, Shakthi Ganesha and many more constitute an impressive variety of iconographic forms. Although they strictly adhere to the *Aagamas*, the contemporary artist has exploited his creative ability to create many Ganeshas, unique to our times. Popular local cults, such as those of Karumaariamman, Mookambika, Kali and Mariamman are new subjects for bronze casting. It is interesting to see how iconographic rules for Shakthi images are adapted to portray these goddesses, whose forms are not mentioned in the ancient texts.

The method used is still that of cire perdue, with the emphasis both on the careful detailing of the clay figure as well as on the final chiselling of the metal.

Apart from the classical bronzes, Tamilnadu also has a separate substratum of folk bronzes, particularly from Thanjavur and Salem. These are much smaller and include figures of animals, sometimes with their riders, and small local deities, particularly female figures. The folk bronzes lack the skilled precision of the Chola figures and generally consist of a metal cast on a rough clay model. The details are chiselled later, but these are hardly noteworthy.

The distinguishing feature of the folk bronzes is their strong resemblance to terracotta figures, emphasising the fact that the latter provided the original inspiration. While the established schools of bronze craftsmanship, spurred on by their royal patrons, went on to produce great works of art, the folk bronzes continued as a village craft. These are used as lamps, votive offerings, temple decorations and even as toys. Their charm lies in their earthy simplicity, their very real depictions of rural life and beliefs, punctuated with a mild abstraction that only village art can produce.

The bronze *uthsavamurthis* taken out in procession around the town fostered several other crafts, such as the making of wooden chariots (*rathas*) and vehicles (*vaahanas*), appliqué cloth decorations, garland-making and flower decorations, the manufacture of intricate jewellery and gold and silver *kavachams* (covering plates made of beaten metal). While the others were renewable, the bronzes alone were permanent. It is fortunate that the system of popular fairs continues to give people an occasion to view the bronzes, as well as to keep alive the bronze-casting industry. Today, the bronzes of Tamilnadu have far outgrown their role within the confines of the temple, and they are to be found adding touches of beauty to homes, offices and public areas.

Metalware

As with bronze casting, brass and copper metalware also have a rich and ancient tradition in Tamilnadu. The objects serve both religious and secular needs, as in the case of lamps, incense burners, utensils, nutcrackers and storage jars and boxes. However, utility is always the primary consideration, and no decoration can interfere with that aspect. The decorations may be secular or religious, from acrobats carved on the handles of nutcrackers to religious symbols crowning the lamps. Although cast by *sthapathis* (sculptors) according to certain norms, there is no stereotyping or uniformity, and the metalware testifies to the craftsman's varied skills.

Due to the large quantities in which the metalware is made, moulds are generally used for smaller items. The larger items may be cast, beaten or forged. A noteworthy form of art metalware in Tamilnadu is the beaten metal repousse , which has resulted in exquisite ornamentation.

The *deepam* or lamp is the best known of Tamilnadu's metalware. Considered to be the symbol of Agni (the god of fire) and Surya (the sun), the lamp is deemed auspicious. From the entry into the world of every human being to his exit, the lamp stands guard heightening the solemnity of the occasion, be it anniversary, initiation or holy wedlock. Its important function of giving light imparted sanctity to the lamp.

The early lamps of stone and shell became terracotta and metal lamps. The earliest shape of the body of the lamp was that of a bowl with a beak at the side for a wick. The *Shilpa Shaastras* (canons of sculpture) devote one full chapter to the characteristics, classifications and production of lamps. It is prescribed that these lamps should have pedestals, for "Mother Earth is accustomed to undergo all sorts of sufferings, but she will not put up with the heat of the lamps". Thus the lamps of Tamilnadu were supported by pedestals or stands, through which the artist expressed his creativity. In due course, the pedestal became an integral part of the lamp, which gave rise to new concepts such as the *vriksha-deepam* (tree lamp).

The variety of lamps in Tamilnadu is almost endless and each is characterised by its peculiar shape and use. They are generally grouped under standing lamps, *aarathi* (votive) lamps, *deepalakshmi*, hand lamps, and chain lamps.

The standing lamps are known as *kuthu-vilakku*. Consisting of a round five-wicked bowl balanced on a slim pedestal standing on a heavy base to prevent accidents and to catch the drippings, these lamps are for domestic use, though they are also used on ceremonial occasions. There are wedding lamps of this type with tiers up to seven branches each, with each branch ending in a similar five-wicked bowl, thus giving out sometimes about 100 flames to a single pedestal.

The most common decoration on the top of the *kuthu-vilakku* is the *hamsa* or mythical swan, but various religious figures and symbols are also popular.

The *aarathi* or votive lamps are generally small in size and are held by the devotee or the priest. The handle is carved like a cobra, fish, peacock, monkey, and in many more shapes. The number of wicks varies from 1 to 251.

To the accompaniment of prayers and *shlokas* (chants) the *aarathi* lamp may be used in the temple, or in the daily *pooja* of the household.

The *deepalakshmi* or *paavai-vilakku*, a common type of temple lamp, is in the form of a female figure holding a shallow bowl which contains the

Opposite page

Sheet metal work, Thanjavur

The design is drawn on thin pieces of copper and silver sheet and beaten out from the back, giving an effect of relief. The sheets are then attached to a brass base.

Following page

Kitchenware shop

A typical village or small town shop selling a wide range of metal kitchenware and other items.

oil and wick. This form is characteristically Tamilian, and can be seen in almost every temple. A male figure carrying a light, however, is very rare. There are several inscriptions recording the endowment of *deepalakshmis* in South Indian temples in historical times, with provisions such as land grants for lighting them. In North India, lamps with human motifs are found only in Bengal, to a limited extent, and even those figures are southern derivatives. *Deepalakshmis* wear a loose saree over a tight-fitting lower garment. In rare cases, the figure stands on an elephant base.

The hand lamps lack pedestals, have larger and deeper bowls, and the back is usually decorated with religious symbols. Gajalakshmi (the goddess Lakshmi flanked on either side by elephants) and lamps with parrots on the rim of the bowl are the most common hand lamps to be found in Hindu homes. These have been adapted by Indian Catholics and Muslims to bear the cross and crescent moon respectively.

Hanging lamps consist of elaborately-decorated bowls suspended by chains. The bowl may be a Gajalakshmi or Ganesha *deepam*, and the chain is embellished with ornamental female figures at regular intervals. These lamps consist of a pan containing the oil with a v-shaped extension to hold the loose wick in place. The upright extension of the back serves as a handle and reflector. In the case of chain lamps, the oil container is sometimes placed above the level of the wick, with the oil trickling down through a small opening into the bowl. These lamps were designed to be hung from arches, and they are decorated with birds and beasts of several species. The flow of the oil to the wick is through an intricately designed siphon concealed within the container. In addition to the lamps, cans in different shapes were made of hammered brass for storing and replenishing the oil.

Incense burners are primarily of two types — a simple bowl with a long handle, or a bowl with a lid. The lower section of the latter contains the fire and incense and the perforated cover allows the fumes to escape. These burners are made of brass or copper, usually adorned with the lotus or other floral designs.

Sheet metalwork

The gold *kavacham* or sheet metal work covering the *vimaana* of the Chidambaram temple.

The utensils of Tamilnadu, once made of perishable materials like clay and stone, consist of numerous jars and pots. Many of the shapes and designs found in excavations from early times continue till today. These utensils can be divided into two major groups: those used for rituals and those used for secular purposes.

With the increasing importance of the temple, the rituals required their own vessels. The *abhishekham* (consecration) of a *saaligraamam* in the case of Vishnu temples, and of a *spatika linga*, in the case of Shiva temples, is performed from a metal bowl. The collection of water has a small separate metal cup with a projection on one side. Vessels for the various ceremonies, such as the ritual bath and the morning, noon, evening and night *pooja*, called for different sizes and shapes, some of which are intricately carved. Thus, for storing water, the temples used very big vessels like the *andaa* and *gangaalam*, with geometric designs near the rim.

For worship conducted in the house by the *yajamaana* (householder), utensils such as the *panchapaathra* (cup) and *uddharani* (spoon) came to play a major role. Vaishnavite or Shaivite marks were etched on some *uddharanis*. The Brihadeeshvara temple in Thanjavur has a wonderful 10th century painting of the kitchen and its vessels.

Cooking utensils also come in many different shapes and sizes. These are usually made of brass, an alloy of copper and zinc, while water is boiled and stored in copper, known for its medicinal properties. Either hammered into shape from sheet brass, sheet copper, or country brass, the vessels are cast in moulds or partly cast and partly beaten. Sheet brass (except scrap) or sheet copper is never melted and made into cast articles, but is always beaten into shape and joined if an article is to be made out of several pieces.

Interestingly, many shapes of the smaller and simpler vessels can be traced to nature, such as the various gourds and flowers. Very few vessels are given handles, and even the larger ones, used for carrying water, are meant to be balanced on the hip, as carrying them by the rim is virtually unknown. Large utensils used in the temples or at

Opposite page

Copper sheet metal work of Veerabhadra in folk style.

Folk deities are earthy and elemental lacking the sophistication of classical sculpture.

Courtesy: Shri Poornaya Achari Muthunai-kanpatti

Left

The making of *urulis*

Top

Common cooking utensil

An *uruli,* a commonly used flat, wide-mouthed dish used for preparing quick- cooling sweets.

Karumari Amman, the Goddess of Thiruverkadu

A folk deity whose worship has become very popular in recent times, this image is an example of how non-cononical forms are adapted to suit *shastraic* requirements of sculpture

Courtesy : Poom Puhar

Copper plate with inscription

It was a common practice to have an etching made of the family deity and a prayer with the name of the family or family head etched out below. This was kept in the family prayer room and worshipped with great honour.

(Courtesy : Mrs. Lilli Vijayaraghavan)

Opposite page

Ceremonial conch

The simple conch, blown on ceremonial occasions, is embellished with metal decorations to add to its beauty.

(Courtesy : Development Centre for Musical Instruments, Madras)

Musical instrument, metal and hide

The *panchamukhavaadyam*, a "five-faced" or five-top percussion instrument flanked by two *kudamuzhaa*. This is a very rare instrument made of metal and is played at the Thiruvarur temple.

(Courtesy : Development Centre for Musical Instruments, Madras).

weddings have two rings near the rim through which a pole is balanced on the shoulders of two men. The shapes are dictated by the use. Water vessels and those used for preserving heat (such as rice cookers) have large bodies and narrow necks, while utensils used for vegetables, sweets, storage and serving have wide brims.

Each utensil has a special name and a special use. The *kudam* fetches water, the *gangaalam* and *andaa* store it. Rice is cooked in a *thavalai*, and its liquid accompaniment in a *chutti paanai*. Sweets are made in flat, wide-mouthed utensils known as *urulis* which permit quick cooling and hardening. Each dish has a separate ladle or *ka- randi* for stirring and serving, its shape and length determined by the item of food. Thus rice is served with a flat *karandi*, the *saambaar karandi* terminates in a small cup, and the milk *karandi* has a small pot at the serving end.

The utensils of the Muslims do not differ from those of the Hindus in the mode of manufacture and technique, though the Muslims use more copper and the Hindus more brass. The shapes of the utensils used by Muslims, however, exhibit a pronounced Persian influence, such as long spouts and trays with arabesque work and the crescent motif.

The brass vessel is cast over a solid clay model covered and turned on a hand lathe with a layer of prepared wax. The turned model is again co- vered with a thick layer of clay in which a small hole is drilled through which the melted wax is re- moved and the molten metal poured in. This takes the place of the wax and the clay is re- moved to finish the article.

Areca nut boxes and nutcrackers have provided ample scope for creativity. It has been said that the habit of chewing *paan* or betel leaf was brought to India, particularly to Tamilnadu, at a very early date, from the East Indian archipelago, where areca nut is very popular. It is the custom in Tamilnadu to welcome the guest by offering betel leaves, a few slices of areca nut, and a little lime. An Ayurvedic treatise called the *Sushruta Samhita* refers to *paan*-chewing, a practice that has resulted in the production of decorated con- tainers. Made of bronze or sheet brass, the boxes

Bottom, left

Garuda

Garuda with an incense holder decorated with a *yaali* (mythical lion) and bells. The range of items in metal is amazing.

(Courtesy : Aparna Art Gallery, Madras)

Top

Sacred tattoos

Samaashrayanam Mudrai or tattoos of the *shankha* (conch) and *chakra* (wheel) used by Tamil Vaishnavas when ordained by the guru.

(Courtesy : Madras Museum)

Toy elephant with rider, mounted on wheels

(Courtesy : Rani Arts & Crafts, Madras)

Metalware 65

Left

Deepam, lamp

The *vriksha-deepam* or tree lamp, consisting of branches coming out of the main pedestal of the standing *hamsa deepam*.

(Courtesy : Poompuhar, Nachiarkoil)

A hand lamp to be placed in the wall niches of houses

It is made of cast brass, and the decoration indicates the religious preferences of the householder. In this case, the figure is that of Gaja Lakshmi

Courtesy : Rani Arts & Crafts, Madras

Nutcrackers of varying designs
(Courtesy : Madras Museum)

Bottom
***Aruvaamanai,* vegetable cutter**

have several small cups or partitions to hold betel, lime and other ingredients. Space is also provided for accommodating the nutcrackers. The nutcracker used to slice the areca nut is made in a variety of ingenious shapes, with animals, birds, flowers, and human figures forming the handles.

Before the advent of plastics, the traditionally long-haired women of Tamilnadu used metal combs, usually made of brass, with two or three long prongs. Wooden combs with several prongs were also used. The top of the comb was fashioned in the form of a female figure or animal, usually an antelope. Perfume was stored in metal containers decorated with *yaali* and *hamsa* designs.

Trays or shallow dishes made of brass—circular, hexagonal, octagonal or oval—are widely used in Tamilnadu. These are found in the temple as well as in the household. Their surfaces are generally not flat, but bear relief figures representing Shaivite or Vaishnavite themes, geometrical patterns and flowers. The trays hold flowers, sweets, sugar, *kumkum*, turmeric and sandalwood paste. Other household and temple prayer items made of metal include the *samaashrayanam mudrai* or tattoos used by Vaishnavas, the Kannan *paadam* or feet of Lord Krishna, the *sadari* or feet used to bless the worshipper and the *shodashopachaaram*, items used in daily ritual.

The popular Thanjavur art plates feature designs of deities, birds, flowers, and geometric patterns beaten out from the back of copper and silver sheets. These are then encrusted on a brass tray, pot (*kudam*) or cup (*panchapaathra*). Generally, the designs follow a theme, such as the *dashaavathaaras* of Vishnu or the miracles of Shiva. Formerly used for making ritual objects, this work is now restricted to wall hangings, which depict a deity made of silver in the centre and alternating copper and silver designs around the rim. A more elaborate form of this art is to be seen in the *kavacham* or coverings of the deity and the temple *vimaana* (spire). The design is drawn on the sheet metal and inwrought, some simply etched and others deeply cut.

Metal toys are chiefly made of brass, neatly polished and attractively finished. They are usually models of horses, cows, or elephants, sometimes

with a mounted figure, sometimes with an *ambaari* (howdah) or platform on which a small image may be placed. Most of the older toys are carefully modelled, but today's mass requirements have resulted in crude workmanship.

Metalware is as old as the megaliths of Tamilnadu, and perhaps even older. This long tradition has maintained the old combination of strength and beauty. The variety of metals used—brass, copper, bronze, bellmetal, silver and gold—is matched by the wide range of shapes and designs. The pragmatism of the Tamilian has always emphasised the utilitarian aspect but, within these parameters, the metal craftsman creates exciting nutcrackers, elegant utensils, and fascinating toys.

Above

Betel holder

Betel holder with two spikes attached to a handle consisting of the figure of a man with legs apart, while two women spring out of his sides. They probably represent acrobats.

(Courtesy : Madras Museum)

Left

Bronze image of a female figure, probably the Mother Goddess, from Adichchanallur, 700 B.C.

Bronze casting has been known in Tamilnadu from very early times.

Courtesy : Madras Museum

Tamilnadu is renowned for the pinnacle of excellence reached in the beauty and elegance of stone-set jewellery.

The origin of the use of jewellery goes back to the very dawn of civilisation, when primitive man and woman, taking a cue from the flora and fauna around them, decorated themselves with reeds, flowers, feathers, and beads carved out of wood, stone and bone. Shells, berries, wings of butterfiles and beetles were all used with great ingenuity. With the advance of civilisation, the materials changed to copper, ivory, agate and semi-precious stones, and later to silver, gold and precious stones.

Nowhere in the world has jewellery formed such an important part of adornment as in India, continuously and through thousands of years. Although, in unsettled periods of Indian history, jewellery became a means of putting by savings and has been a method of providing property to daughters in the form of sthree-dhana, the love of jewellery in India is really an expression of the aesthetic impulse of the people and their joy in the creation of beauty.

This love of ornaments can be traced to our tribal heritage, as evidenced by the flower, bird and fish motifs which are predominant to this day. In Tamilnadu, for example, flowers encrusted with stones dominate jewellery designs. Leaves of the sacred pipal (bo) tree, the betel leaf, jasmine buds, the lotus, the shembagappoo (the champa or frangipani) and chrysanthemum form the basic design of most ornaments. Equally popular are the peacock, parrot and swan.

The ancient origin of jewellery in Tamilnadu can be seen from the sculptures and carvings in temples, a veritable cornucopia of the jeweller's art. Most of the figures of men and women are scantily clad, but of jewellery, from head to toe, there is no dearth.

Ancient Tamil literature abounds in references to jewellery. The Silappadikaaram (The Epic of the Anklet) is based on a story built around the anklet of Kannagi, wife of Kovalan. Puhar, where they lived, is described as a city of wealth, abounding in jewels of gold, pearls and precious stones. Jewellers were held in such high regard that the main street of Puhar was occupied by them and they lived and worked there.

The jewels of the courtesan, Madhavi, who lured Kovalan, are described in great detail. She wore a peeli, a jewel worn on the third toe to this day. She had ornaments encircling her thighs, and around her waist was a belt of 32 strands of large pearls. Her armlets were encrusted with pearls, and her bracelets with precious stones. Her forearms tinkled with bangles of different types — gold bangles, navarathna bangles (nine-stone bangles called pariyakam in those days), conch and coral bangles. She also wore a ring shaped like the mouth of an open fish (this inverted v-shaped ring, the nali, is still worn today). And she had other rings of precious stones and diamonds. Around her neck she wore a necklace of chains and a string of precious gems held together by an ornamental clasp, covering the nape. She wore serrated earrings set with alternating diamonds and emeralds. On her head were two different ornaments, one on either side, the kind of jewels worn even by present-day brides and dancers.

Opposite page

A jeweller at work

The basic design is made of gold base and the stones fitted in.

Neck ornaments

Front (see jacket) and back of a *maangaa-maalai*, a necklace of gold mangoes, stone-studded in *kundan* work, typical of the heavy neckwear of Tamilnadu. The pendant has either a lotus centre, stone-encrusted peacocks, or creepers with a flower shaped centre. This jewel is usually a family hairloom worn by the bride and is also popularly worn by Bharatha Natyam dancers who consider themselves the brides of the temple deity.

Through thousands of years, the jewellery of Tamilnadu progressed from its tribal heritage to greater sophistication and elegance. However, it is obvious that even as far back as the Sangam era, it had reached the height of excellence and refinement, and the designs and ornaments of today's traditional stone-set gold jewellery are practically the same as those worn two millennia ago. Different pieces of jewellery adorned each part of the body, literally from head to toe. Each ornament was designed to fit into and blend with the shape of the body, following the lines of the body or limb, as if carved into the part adorned by the jewel.

The Tamils, having been great seafaring people and traders from the very dawn of history, were familiar with gems imported from beyond the seas, even before the Christian era. The Tamil *kuruvindam*, from which the English corundum (denoting ruby and sapphire) is derived, indicates its ancient Tamil heritage. Marco Polo, writing in the 13th century, speaks of the kings of the Coromandel country (the eastern coast of Tamilnadu), describing one of them as wearing golden bracelets set with the richest pearls, necklaces of rubies, emeralds and sapphire, anklets, at his feet and gold rings on his toes. He wore a rosary of 104 large rubies and pearls.

The missionary Abbé Dubois, in his account of this region, mentions that even men wore ear ornaments and ascetics (*sanyaasis*) also wore them for health reasons (though they used copper to show their non-attachment to gold or wealth). The belief in piercing the ears for health reasons has been prevalent since ancient times.

With the advent of nose jewellery in the medieval period (probably brought in by the Muslim invaders), gold worn on pierced nostrils was believed to cure sinus infection and head colds. The seeds of the *rudraaksham* (*uthrasam*) tree, often decorated with gold clasps, are used even today as a rosary during worship. They are believed to be beneficial in controlling blood pressure.

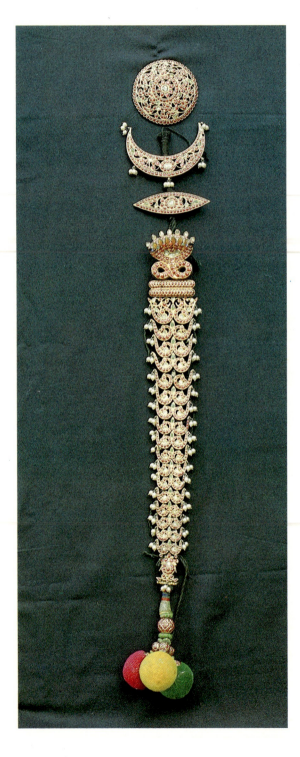

Left

Jadanaagam hair ornament

Below the *raakkodi* commences the *jadanaagam* or hair-serpent symbolic of Anantha, the serpent on which lies Lord Vishnu. It commences with a stone-set crescent moon. Below this is a piece similar to the *thaazhambu* flower. After this is the actual *jadanaagam*, the most elaborate hair-jewel of India. It is attached to braided or plaited hair which is alwaya likened to the coils of a serpent. At the beginning of the braid is the ruby and diamond-studded many-headed cobra, Anantha, with rows of coils which serve as the couch of Vishnu. The hair-piece attached to the braid is of descending thickness and is shaped like the buds of the fragrant jasmine flower. The pieces are interlaced in such a way that the jewel is supple and enfolds the braided hair. At the lower end of the braided is the *kunjalam* or *jadaguchchu* of three tassets topped by gold-encrusted bells. This jewel is brilliant, outstanding and the pinnacle of sophistication.

Raakodi, a hair ornament

On the back of the head is worn the *raakkodi*, about 6 cm in diameter, stone encrusted, with a *hamsa* or swan in the centre. The swan has several connotations in Hindu mythology. It typifies grace and beauty. It is also believed that the swan has the ability to separate water from milk, spitting out the former and drinking the latter. Similarly, it is believed that the evolved human being should separate evil and good. The *raakkodi* is set in *kundan* work (similar to the *kundan* setting of Rajasthan) using 24-carat gold at the bottom and 22-carat gold on top. The gold is worked in the method known as *izhuppu-velai* where the gold is etched and stones set in this base. The rubies used are cabochon rubies also known as *kuruvincam* stones.

Bridal decorations

Thalaisaamaan are bridal decorations worn on the head. The predominant stone is the ruby, interspersed with uncut diamonds and pearls. One part of this jewel is worn along the centre parting and is held in place by a second matching jewel worn on either side of the brow on the hair-line. On top of the head on either side are stone-set figures of the sun and the crescent moon, the former a symbol of a brilliant marriage and the latter symbolic of peace and calm.

Royal necklace

A five-strand gold bead *nellikkaai mani-maalai* usually worn by temple deities or rulers.

Opposite page

Elaborately carved gold pendant

On the clasp is a carved figure of Shiva as Nataraja, the lord of dance. In the centre of the pendant is *nagaas* — gold carved work with the figures of Shiva or Maheshwara and Parvati as Uma, riding on Nandi, the bull. They are flanked on either side by *apsaras* or celestial figures, flying through the heavens. On the bottom of the pendant are two ruby-set *pulinagams* or tiger claws, between which is a ruby lotus pendant. Tiger claws are worn for luck and are also symbolic of strength and power.

Balakrishna, the child Krishna, with Yashoda a popular theme in Thanjavur paintings

A repousse effect is created by gold-leaf gesso work studded with pearls, glass and semi-precious stones.

Courtesy : Nanditha Krishna

Another belief still prevalent is in the efficacy of the *navarathna* or nine sacred gems in controlling the nine planets. The origin of this belief goes back to the worship of Murugan, the main deity worshipped by the Tamils, also known as Skanda, Karthikeya or Subrahmanya. The ancient text, the *Skandapuraana*, has a charming story of how these nine stones became so powerful.

The *devas*, celestial beings, approached Lord Shiva for help in destroying the demon Padmasura, who was harassing them. Shiva, in his anger against the demon, opened his third eye, out of which fiery sparks blazed forth. Frightened by this sight, Parvati ran away from Shiva, and as she did so her tinkling anklets broke and the nine gems embedded in them scattered in all directions. When Shiva reassumed his peaceful aspect, he saw a different form of his beloved Parvati in each of the nine stones and, through his divine powers, he created nine warriors out of them to assist his son Karthikeya (Murugan) in destroying the demon.

These nine gems are considered so powerful that they are worn to this day to enhance the powers of a beneficial planet or to minimise the ill-efects of a malefic planet. The nine stones usually associated with the planets are the ruby (for Ravi, the sun), pearl (for Chandra, the moon), coral (for Kuja or mars), topaz (for Guru or Jupiter), diamond (for Shukra or Venus), sapphire (for Sani or Saturn), zircon (for Rahu) and cat's eye (for Ketu). A *navarathna* ring consisting of all nine stones is considered especially efficacious, but great care is taken to see that the stones are placed in a particular order, each one having a special position.

Gold worn on the body, especially when bathing, was believed to have medicinal properties. In fact gold was, and is, so highly regarded that it is never demeaned by being worn on the feet, where it can be soiled. Only kings and icons in temples were permitted to wear gold anklets.

The ornaments of Tamilnadu, southern Karnataka and Andhra Pradesh have many similarities. Although there are individual pieces unique to each region, others like the *oddiyaanam* (gold waist belt), *vanki* (armlet), and *jimikki* (ear-drop) are common to all parts of South India.

Starting with jewellery worn on the head, the elaborate *thalaisaamaan* is a bridal decoration. Since the *devadaasis* or temple dancers of old considered themselves brides of the temple deity, they wore a bride's jewels while dancing. This tradition still continues and has resulted in South Indian bridal jewellery being mistakenly called Bharatha Natyam dance jewellery.

The thalaisaamaan consists of heavy stone-set jewellery, with rubies or red stones predominating, but interspersed with emeralds and uncut diamonds. One piece of this jewel is worn on the centre parting and another tied along the hair-line on the forehead, Decorative pieces shaped like the sun and the moon are worn on either side of the head to invoke the blessings of these celestial beings, the sun for good health, brilliance and power, the moon for romance and a life of peace and calm.

The decoration of the hair does not stop with the front and top of the head. On the back of the head is worn the *naagar*, a five-headed snake in gold or a *raakkodi* (or *raakkadi*), a circular piece, stone-encrusted with a swan in the centre. When a *jadanaagam* (literally meaning hair-serpent) is worn, the *raakkodi* is followed by a stone-set crescent moon and a third piece shaped like the fragrant *thaazhambu* (screw pine) flower.

Then commences the actual *jadanaagam*, the most elaborate jewel found anywhere in India for hair decoration. Worn on plaited hair, it is a jewel now practically extinct. A woman's crowning glory, her hair, has been the subject of flights of fancy by Indian poets — they liken the raven tresses slithering down in a plaited braid to a serpent.

The *jadanaagam* proper commences with a ruby and diamond studded many-headed divine cobra, Anantha, with rows of coils (the latter serves as the couch of Lord Vishnu).

This is followed by a hair-piece of diminishing thickness consisting of flowers and buds cleverly interlaced, so that the jewel is soft and supple and appears to be a part of the braided hair. At the narrow lower end burst out three tassels (*kunjalam* or *jadaguchchu*), topped by gold-encrusted bells. The whole effect of this jewel is extremely dramatic.

Another unusual ancient hair ornament is the *shevarikottai*, a golden buckle used to attach an artificial switch of hair to the chignon. For plaited hair not decorated with a *jadanaagam*, a circular *thirugusaamanthi poo*, also called a *thirugu poo*, is worn in the middle of the braid. It is made either of diamonds, red stones or plain gold, depending on the wearer's wealth. Jewellery is literally worn from the cradle. The *uchchippooteeka* is a small lotus-shaped ornament worn by little boys and girls on top of the head on the right side. Believed to be a copy of the jewel worn by the child Krishna, this is another piece practically extinct now.

There are several kinds of jewellery to adorn the ear. In the deep southern districts of Tamilnadu, older women enlarge the hole in the ear lobe by wearing rolled palm leaves which are made larger and larger, increasing the size of the hole to nearly three centimetres in diameter. A *paambadam*, a jewel of six earrings of different shapes, is then worn, dragging the ear half-way down to the shoulder.

Men in rural areas even today wear ear-studs of single stones called *kadukkan*. The normal ear jewel of women consists of ear-studs, lotus-shaped, of rubies or diamonds, called the *kammal*. Below this hangs the *jimikki*, a bell-shaped ear-drop, either in gold or stonestudded. Sometimes another ear-drop, a *lolaakku*, is worn which can be of any design, though usually it has a floral motif.

A beautiful jewel is the *maattal* of gold or pearls attached at the lower end of the *kammal* and hooked on to the hair above the ear. Its purpose is to support the weight of the ornaments.

Jewellery worn on the outer and inner ear had gone out of fashion but is coming back amongst the young. They are the *kathribaavali*, the *kuruthubaavali* and the *koppu*. The *jilpaabaavali*, a pendant worn on the hair above the ear and falling below the hairline is now extinct.

The jewel most commonly worn on the nose, on the left or right side, just above the nostril, is the single stone *mookkupottu*. The *besari* (of eight diamonds) worn on the left side of the nose is balanced by the *muthu* (consisting of a large diamond with three diamonds hanging loosely below it) on the right side. More popular with young girls is the *hamsa besari*, shaped like a swan and stone-studded, and worn on the right side. Very popular with dancers is the *nathu*, a stone-studded ring pierced through the left nostril.

Another nose jewel which appeared in the south for the first time around the 17th century is the *bullaakku*. This diamond-studded jewel is suspended from the pierced central

Opposite page, left

Armlet

The inverted v-shaped *vanki* is a jewel worn on the upper arm which fits without any strain to the wearer. This jewel goes back to *naaga* or snake worship, and the effect of coiled snakes characterises this jewel. The inverted-v effect may also be brought out by two parrots or two peacocks on either side with a flower pendant in the centre.

Opposite page, right

Ear jewellery

Ear jewellery consists of the lotus-shaped *kammal* of diamonds or rubies worn on the lower lobe of the ear. Below this hangs the bell-shaped ear jewel called the *jimikki*, set in coloured stones with pearls hanging at the lower end. From the *kammal* is attached the *maattal* which is hooked on to the hair above the ear and supports the weight of the ear jewellery. The *maattal* can be of plain stones, gold, or elaborate with pearls and stone-studded parrots. An old jewel coming back into fashion is a small *kadukkan*, for which a second hole is pierced in the lower ear.

Gold belt, now worn by dancers

The *oddiyaanam*, or waist-belt, is worn tight around the waist as it is believed that this keeps the waist slim. A sign of beauty for women is a narrow waist accentuated by large hips. The *oddiyaanam* can be of silver or gold, or stone-encrusted with *mogappu* of flower designs. This *oddiyaanam*, with ruby-encrusted peacocks, is of particular beauty.

A Kuravan (gypsy) wearing red and black beads, known as *kurathi mani* (gypsy beads)

The silver pendant encases tiger claws, worn for luck, and to give the wearer the strength of a tiger. Another pendant is a silver amulet (called a *rakshai*) worn as protection against the evil eye, black magic, witch-craft and ill-health. Inside the *rakshai* are *mantrams* or sacred spells for special protection. In the Kuravan's ears are silver rings and beads.

Left

Toda woman in her traditional jewellery

Top

A village woman wearing traditional folk jewellery

The pierced ear is enlarged by older women by wearing rolled palm leaves inside the hole. These rolls are increased every now and then in the early stages. Then a *paambadam*, a jewel of six earrings of different shapes, is fastened on the lower lobe so that it gets larger with the weight of the jewellery which drags the ear-lobe down to the shoulder.

membrane of the nose and falls on the centre of the upper lip ending in a single pearl. Though once worn by all classes and today only by Bharatha Natyam dancers, it was, in the early decades of this century, a symbol of aristocracy, invariably used by women of the upper strata of society and of princely families.

Neck jewellery is a world apart, and the variety is endless. The basic jewel for a married woman is the *thaali* or *mangalasuthra*, the marriage talisman. First tied on string and then replaced by a gold chain, the important part of the *thaali* is the pendant, whose design is determined by the community to which the woman belongs. It could be a *thulasi* (holy basil) plant, the conch and discus of Vishnu, or it could be heavily stone-studded as worn by Chettinad women.

The traditional *addigai* is a necklace of large cabochon rubies set in ascending order ending in a lotus-shaped pendant. Today it is often set with diamonds which, however, can never compete with the beauty of the red-stoned *kempaddigai*.

The necklace of mangoes, the *maangaamaalai*, consists of stone-studded gold mangoes strung together with a huge pendant of encrusted peacocks. This has now become part of the Bharatha Natyam, dance costume.

Strings of pearls with large stone-studded pendants have been popular from time immemorial, as pearls are found in the seas off Tuticorin and pearl-diving was once a lucrative trade. In ancient India it was believed that flawless pearls prevented misfortune. They were therefore worn by princes and became part of a bride's trousseau. Often, a gold amulet enclosing sacred words formed the pendant of a pearl necklace. Equally strong was the belief in the power of a tiger's claw in preventing ill-luck. These claws were set in gold, framed with stones and made into neck ornaments.

Besides gold chains of various designs, the gold-coin-necklace, the *kaasumaalai*, is typical of this region, the size and weight of the

Marriage necklace

Thaalis of the Chettiar women which are distinct from those of others. The design of the *thaali* depends on the caste or family traditions.

Opposite page top and bottom

Silver *golusu* or anklets

Heavy and decorative, the anklets hardly make any sound, silence is associated with female modesty.

coins depending on the wealth of the wearer. The *salangai* are gold beads strung together interspersed with black or coral beads. The gold *kanti* and the ruby *rathna kanti* are necklaces worn on festive occasions. The *asili* (known in North India as the *haasli*) is a stiff stone-set necklace which is believed to be a protection for the wearer's collar-bone.

Of the jewels worn on the upper arm, the inverted-V-designed *vanki* is the most beautiful, some very elaborately inlaid with stones, others of pure gold. An effect of coiled snakes is often part of this jewel, tracing its origin to snake or *naaga* worship. The inverted-v effect may be achieved by two parrots or two peacocks carved on either side. The *vanki* is so beautifully designed that it fits over the arm without any strain to the wearer.

The *naagavathu* is an armlet of gold with a stone-studded crest in the centre; the name derives from its appearance of a serpent encircling the arm. The *kadayam* is an armlet worn by young girls.

There is a wide range of bangles or *valai* and *kankanam* either of gold or set with stones. *Gettikkaappu* are plain gold bracelets worn tight around the wrist, and the *thoda* is a bracelet with a stone-set crest.

Matching the *vanki* is the inverted v-shaped ring called the *nali*, unique to South India. It is presented to a bride, usually by her maternal aunt.

Another jewel unique to the south is the waist belt, the *oddiyaanam*, worn tight around the waist. Plain silver or gold belts used to be worn all the time by women as they were believed to keep the waist slim. Also, narrow waists accentuated the hips, this being a sign of beauty in Tamil culture. *Oddiyaanams* with stone-encrusted centers or *mogappus* are of a wide range, each rivalling the other in beauty.

On the feet are worn *golusu* or silver anklets. *Puduchcheri golusu* of a chain design hail from Pondicherry. *Gajja golusu* are heavy anklets with bells that tinkle. *Thandai* are stiff

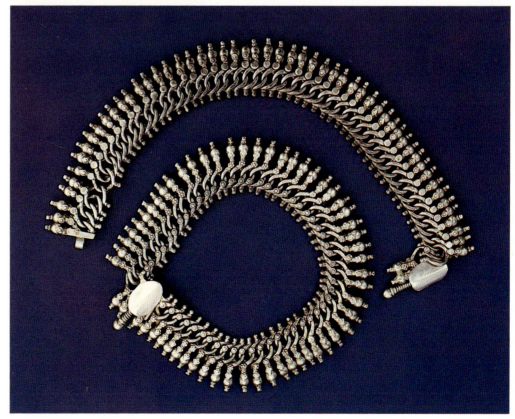

anklets with bells inside which also tinkle and add to the graceful movements of the wearer. A plain stiff anklet, the *kaal kaappu* protects the ankle of the wearer and was believed to be necessary for children to wear.

On the toes, again, only silver is worn. On the second toe are worn the heavy silver *metti*, two on each foot, which produce a musical sound as they strike the floor. To keep the *metti* in place is the *siththu*, made of two rows of silver wires and worn tight on the toe. The *peeli* is designed like a crest and is worn on the third toe.

The great Indian concept of *R'ta* or cosmic order is integrated into the jewellery of Tamilnadu. This has resulted in perfect symmetry in the designs of ornaments — what is on the left side of a jewel is mirror-matched on the right side. There is never any discordance.

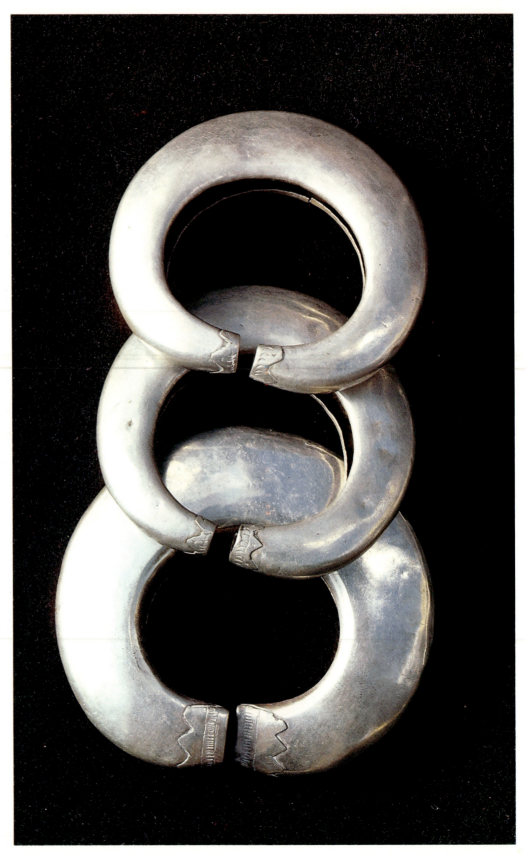

Even the rare cases of assymmetry in the shape of two different ornaments, is gracefully balanced, as in the case of the *nathu* on one side of the nose and the *besari* on the other.

Jewellery in Tamilnadu has always had closed settings, with stones deeply embedded in gold. Open-setting work is virtually unknown. A three-dimensional effect is achieved with the use of wax, which forms the base over which the design is fashioned in gold and the stones encrusted. Thus the jewellery appears heavier than it actually is.

Tribes such as the Todas, Badagas and Kotas of the Nilgiris wear silver and other metal jewellery. The items include bracelets, earrings and necklaces. The ornaments are huge and heavy, and intricately carved. A popular Toda jewel is a necklace with pendants of bent wires. Shells are also used for making jewels. The Kadar tribe of the Aanamalais have less intricate work and use a variety of beads. But the greatest variety of beads, made of seeds,

fruits, glass, and wood are to be found among the gypsies of Tamilnadu, the Nari Kuravas, whose livelihood depends on the sale of these beads to rural children.

Unlike many other parts of India, elaborate jewellery is still worn in Tamilnadu. But it is unfortunate that polished stones are replacing uncut diamonds, rubies, sapphires, and emeralds, and Western designs in necklaces are invading the market, destroying a rich heritage in jewellery rarely seen anywhere else in the world. However, it is hoped that the innate grace of the people, their love of beauty, elegance and refinement will prevail, and will not be lost in the maelstrom of modernisation.

Opposite page, left

Close-up of Varalakshmi, the goddess worshipped by married women for the long life of their husbands

The face is made of metal, generally silver, occasionally brass or gold, and tied to a coconut placed on a pot. The deity is decorated with traditional jewellery — the *nathu* a large nose-ring, passing through one nostril and a single stone *mookkuthi* on another. From beneath her nose comes the *bullaakku*. She wears a *kathribaavali* on the upper ear lobe and a *thodu* from which hangs a *jimmikki* on the lower lob. Around her neck is a *karugumani*, a black necklace, with a gold *pottu* worn by married women in northern Tamilnadu. The *karugamani* and *bullaakku*, as the worship of Varalakshmi herself , are of Telugu origin and are more prevalent in the northern part of the state, as in North Arcot district which borders Andhra Pradesh.

Opposite page, right

Tribal silver

Silver bangles worn by Toda women of the Nilgiri hills. The Todas are a Dravidian tribe with a distinct language and culture which they have managed to preserve by virtue of their remote situation. Toda jewellery is made of heavy chunky silver in profusion.

Silver necklace of the Todas

Terracottas

Guarding the entrance to every village in Tamilnadu is an enormous terracotta horse, the horse of Ayyanaar, the watchman of the village and the commander of the demon hosts. It is Ayyanaar who protects the village from the evil of drought, disease, enemies and restless departed spirits. Sporting an enormous moustache, fierce teeth and with his eyes wide open to keep vigil, he stands at the entrance to the village or near the water tank, surrounded by his horses and commanders, or *veerans*. He is regarded as a good and benevolent protector, whose ritual is Brahminical in nature and generally eschews animal sacrifice.

Described as the largest terracotta sculptures ever built in the history of mankind, the horses of Ayyanaar range from less than half a metre to over six metres in height. While those at the village entrance are guardians, reflecting Ayyanaar's protective powers, smaller versions are gifted to Ayyanaar as votive offerings by devotees. Apart from horses, Ayyanaar is also surrounded by soldiers, bulls and elephants, the last particularly popular among fishermen.

As pottery is probably the most ancient of crafts, the earliest terracottas in Tamilnadu are human and animal figures from Paiyampalli, dating to a neolithic period between 3000 and 1000 BC. The figures are crude and represent terracotta art in its infancy. Black and red-ware pottery belonging to megalithic sites, dating to a period between 500 BC and AD 100, are found in several places such as Sanur, Amrithamangalam and Kunrathur in Chingleput district. At a related non-megalithic site at Adichanallur in Thirunelveli district, there is a more primitive form of black and red ware.

A rich terracotta site of this period is the Nilgiri hills, which abounds in human and animal figures, both religious and secular. These are hand-moulded either completely or partially and have incised dot impressions on the body. Several parts are made separately and then joined together. Their linear composition renders them static, the only dynamism conveyed by the movement of the hands. Moulded figures were unknown in the early periods.

Between about the third century BC and the fourth century AD, sites such as Arikamedu, Kanchipuram, Thirukkampuliyur, Alagarai, Uraiyur and Kaveripoompattinam produced large quantities of terracotta objects. The figures—religious as well as secular include village deities, *vriksha devathas* (spirits of the trees), *naagalingas*, Vaishnavite and Shaivite deities and their symbols, Buddhist and Jain symbols and figures (especially in Kaveripoompattinam) of women in royal headgear, dancers, men and women, including aborigines, in various poses, head-dresses, garments and ornaments and, finally, terracotta jewellery and musical instruments. The ornamentation on the clay included a myriad of painted designs and incised and appliquéd patterns. Clay vessels were also used as burial urns (*mudumakkai thazhi*) all over the Tamil country.

The art of terracotta-making continues at the same two levels till today. The first is for everyday use in the villages and extends to the making of mud huts and kitchens; and the second, the figures of gods, goddesses, their attendants, votive objects and, most important, the horses.

Terracotta pottery today is generally very simple and only painted at weddings. Salem alone had developed a black pottery. Ranging from water-drawing and storing pots to cooking vessels, their shapes depend on their use. They are given importance during Pongal, the harvest festival heralding the arrival of Utharaayanam, the sun in

the northern hemisphere. On Bhogi, the previous day, the old mud vessels in the house are ritually burnt, symbolising the destruction of the period of darkness. The next day, on the birth of Utharaayanam, the new pots are kept out in the freshly cleaned and, if possible, lime-washed kitchen. The position of prime importance is given to the rice pot, which is decorated with the *vibhoothi* or sacred ash and *kumkum*. A fresh young turmeric plant is tied around the neck of the pot and the top is covered with white cloth. Inside is a combination of rice, lentils, sugarcane and jaggery, symbolising the fruits of the harvest. The dish, also known as *pongal*, is allowed to overflow on to the sides of the pot, indicating a bountiful harvest.

The kitchen is made of clay. On a low platform or *medai*, there is a single stove or *aduppu* and a double stove or *kodi aduppu*, built of brick and clay and fed by wood for fuel. Extra stoves are made up of bricks placed strategically. Even when the mud walls are lime-washed, the *medai* and *aduppu* are left in their natural colour. An important daily ritual is washing the stove and platform, and decorating them with *kolam* or symbolic designs made of rice flour.

Apart from the cooking pots, other terracotta items in the house include large vessels for storing grain, the *thulasi maadam* or decorated platform for the *thulasi* plant, found in every home, and clay toys for the children.

At the wedding of certain castes the ceremonies cannot begin till the potter supplies his vividly painted pots. Coated with a lime base, they are decorated with brightly-painted flora, fauna, Vishnu's wheel and conch and geometric designs. The potter lights terracotta *ahals* or small lamps placed on a wooden stand and performs a *pooja* to the pots. At the potter's wedding this is the most important single ritual. The pots symbolise continuity of life, of creation, destruction and rebirth, as in the fresh creation of pots from old ones.

The potter is a man of importance in an Indian village, for he provides the utensils required in every home. In Tamilnadu the potters are known as the *kuyavar. kulaalar* or *velar*. They trace their origins to the union of a Brahmin man and a Shudra

woman and, often. to Vishwakarma, the divine craftsman himself. Their social position is high and they wear the *poonal* or sacred thread. At village temples, particularly those involving animal sacrifices which are shunned by the Brahmins, the potters officiate as priests. Their importance is due to the fact that they are associated with the life process of the village from birth, when the breaking of the birth sac is symbolised by the pot, till death, when a mud pot is broken at the funeral pyre.

The making of a terracotta figure is of momentous importance beginning at the time when it is first ordered. It may be either a new image, or one specially made for a festival, or the "renewing" of an existing figure. In the last two cases, a handful of the mud used to make the earlier image is put into the new image. The order is given on an auspicious day, while the eyes and other features of the face— the character—are also sculpted on an auspicious day. The figure is brought to the village on the shoulders of the senior male citizens and the celebrations begin, with a lot of noise, fanfare and blood-letting. The potter acts as the *poojaari* or priest, for it is only his touch of the eyes which can confer 'life' on the idol.

Most village deities are made of terracotta. Each village generally has an *ammankovil* or temple to the mother goddess, with a shrine for her male consort, a temple to Pillaiyaar or Ganesha, and the great horses or *kudirais* of Ayyanaar, the *kaaval deivam* or guardian deity of the village.

The most popular *amman* is Maariamman, followed by Kaali. Maariamman is the vindictive and dreaded goddess of disease, particularly small-pox. Both Maariamman and Kaali are propitiated with animal sacrifices, the former with the blood of sheep and fowl and the latter with the blood of buffaloes. Other female deities include the headless *amman*, a form of Parashurama's mother Renuka Devi, whose head is generally replaced by a *kalasham* or pot containing a coconut and mango leaves, and Draupadi *amman*. The Saptha Matrikas are known in Tamilnadu as the seven virgins or sisters, the Saptha Kannigais, Aakaasha Kannigais and Kannimaars. They are the tutelary deities of the water tank and are situated far away from Maariamman. There are several local goddesses such as Kanniamman,

Kuayiamman, Pidaari, Rajrajeshwari, Meenakshi, Karumaari and a host of others.

Most village goddesses are usually worshipped with blood and liquor. As their status is enhanced, they are identified with the consorts of Vishnu and Shiva and the blood sacrifices are replaced by less gory Brahminic rituals. Generally, the village goddesses are primitive-looking terracottas, some times even a mere mound of clay, covered with sandal paste, turmeric and *kumkum* and occasionally painted with earth colours. As the village temple gains money and sophistication, these figures are replaced by stone images. The male deities, sometimes the consorts of these *ammans*, are also made of terracotta. Karuppan, Chittan, Bhairavar (a form of Shiva), Veerabhadra, who severs the head of Daksha (and who, interestingly, has Jain connections), and Madurai Veeran, the popular "hero of Madurai" are among several others. Madurai Veeran sits on a horse, with a raised sword, supported by Muniyaandi, an attendant demon, at the shrine of Maariamman. Both Madurai Veeran and Muniyaandi are disreputable characters propitiated with animal sacrifices. In contrast to the more primitive-looking female figures, the male figures are very powerful and attractive in appearance, made with great care, with strong features and drapery lines and attractive ornamentation.

Another important terracotta shrine is the *naaga* or serpent shrine, situated under a *pipal* tree and near an ant-hill. Made of clay, it reproduces the inter-twined body of a snake and is propitiated for its power of protection and rejuvenation.

Making a terracotta figure involves several days of work for the potter, whose wife and children are his assistants and critics. The moist clay is mixed with straw and sand to achieve the proper consistency. In the case of a horse, it is rolled into four cylinders with a piece of wood. The four cylinders are joined to become the legs, and the body is built up gradually, with rolls of clay, up to the neck. The trimmings, consisting of bells, mirrors, grotesque faces (*kirthimukha*) and sometimes *makaras* (crocodiles) are made separately and joined to the main figure. The bells are supposed to warn miscreants of Ayyanaar's arrival, while the *kirthimukhas* and *makaras* frighten

Opposite page

Potter at work, Thanjavur district

A potter making a grain container, known as the *kuluppai*, at Thribhuvanam in Thanjavur district. This container is made of a mixture of clay and paddy husk.

The making of terracotta horses, Kurthunaikkanpatti, Salem district

The craftsman makes the figures either whole or in part and then fires them in his country kiln, using a simple process of burning straw and dried cow-dung in a makeshift oven surrounded by old terracotta pots.

Isakai Amman, a blood-thirsty goddess of Jain origin

Isakai is a corruption of the word Yakshi. She is dreaded in the countryside around Salem and is generally portrayed with a human being hanging out of her mouth.

Opposite page

Terracotta horse

A horse of Ayyanaar, the guardian spirit of every village, accompanied by *veerans* or "braves", warriors who watch over the village. The horses may range from 60 cm in height to over 10 metres. Originally, they were made of only terracotta. Nowadays, they may be made of either terracotta or stucco, and are painted in bright colours.

them off. The horse's head is made separately and supported by pots and sticks while it dries, to prevent sagging. All the parts are joined together after they dry and on the auspicious tenth day, the image of Ayyanaar, seated on the horse, is given its features, to create the character. The whole is baked in a rustic kiln of unfired pots placed around the figure, fuelled by a combination of straw and *verati* or dried cow-dung, and covered with mud. In the case of large figures, the various parts of the body are made separately and fired, then joined together and fired again. Sometimes the figures are painted, the faces red, denoting anger, and the neck blue denoting calm. The rest of the body and decorations are also painted in vivid colours.

While the earlier Ayyanaars were made along simple lines, the later ones are identified by larger eyeballs and more ferocious brows. As time passed, the eyebrows become straighter and there was an increase of straight and angular lines. Later still, the moustache increased in size and the figures were brightly painted. The oldest Ayyanaars and horses are probably to be found in Salem district.

Today, Salem and Pudukottai Districts are the sites of the manufacture of the large terracotta horses, although the smaller figures—human, divine and animal—are made all over the state. Whereas in the past all terracottas were individually made and fired, the increasing market, particularly for terracotta art items, has resulted in the development and use of moulds.

Sometimes Ayyanaar's horses and commanders are made of stucco. While stucco art faithfully copies the terracotta forms, it has been unable to reproduce its grace and beauty, and the stucco figures have become stiff and lifeless.

Glazed ceramics are a more recent development in Tamilnadu. Karigiri has developed a highly-glazed form of biscuitware, with incised patterns, Persian styles, and a blue or green glaze. Auroville at Pondicherry has created a heavy kiln-dried pottery which resembles stoneware but retains the feel of clay. The traditional figures of the village goddesses and heroes are also produced in rich ceramic colours. Some of the traditional pottery designs have now been developed to make contemporary tableware.

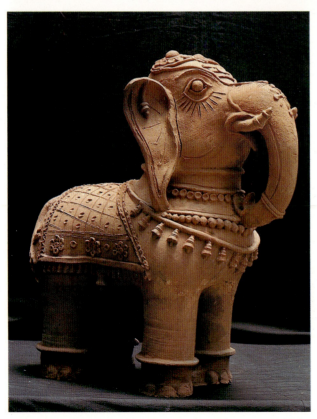

Opposite page, top

Terracotta lamps

Terracotta oil lamps or *deepam* which are small enough to be carried by hand. They are kept in niches built into the walls of the house. The decorations on these lamps indicate the religious and sectarian beliefs of the householder.

Opposite page, bottom left

Terracotta elephant

While the horse is favoured by most villagers, fishermen prefer the elephant as a mount for Ayyanaar.

Opposite page, bottom right

Uruvaram, folk deity

Uruvaram, a terracotta figure of a female who is often kept near babies as a child guardian, to ward off danger and the evil eye. It is given as a votive offering to the temple.

(Courtesy : Gita Ram)

Terracotta Pooranai, a village deity, and one of the consorts of Ayyanaar

(Courtesy : Poompuhar).

Following pages

Vamuni, Shakthimuni and Vallamuni, village deities, in a Muniyappa *kovil* (temple), Thathaiyampatti, near Omalur

Village worship includes worship of several spirits such as these who, it is believed, unless propitiated, can bring disaster to the village.

Vinayaka Chathurthi is an occasion when clay Ganeshas are made and sold in large numbers. Ranging from a few centimetres to a metre in height, they may be glazed, painted, baked, or even unbaked. The last are the most popular, as the figures are lowered into the well on the day after the *pooja*, and the unbaked figures crumble easily. Unlike the enormous Ganeshas made for communal gatherings in Maharashtra, the festival in Tamilnadu is restricted to the home. For the festival, each family buys a Ganesha, which is generally within thirty centimetres in height.

It is interesting to note that, whereas the stone images develop a permanent "life" once consecrated, the terracotta images come to life only for the duration of the festival and lose their powers soon after. The creation of the image, its limited life span and its destruction, leading to yet another creation of an image, represent the birth, life, death and rejuvenation of all nature. Thus terracottas possess a unique position as representative of the life cycle itself.

Opposite page

Glazed ceramics

Karigiri ware, a highly-glazed green ceramic ware decorated with incised patterns. The handles are in the shape of *makaras*.

(Courtesy : Madras Museum).

Black clay pot with lid

This black clay is a speciality of Salem district and such jars are used for storage. Elsewhere, terracottas have retained their red earth colour.

(Courtesy : Gita Ram).

Woodcraft & Musical Instruments

The finest wood carving in Tamilnadu is associated with its temples. It is at its best and most characteristic in processional vehicles for the deities. These are the huge wooden temple cars (*ther*) attached to most larger temples, the numerous mounts (*vaahanas*) and the small pillared shrines (*rathams*) for the deities. Occasionally, beautiful woodcraft is found in the elaborately carved wooden arches, doorways and guardian (*dvaarapaala*) panels at the entrance of the temples.

The traditional woodcarvers and carpenters throughout Tamilnadu, like the stonecutters, silversmiths, goldsmiths and blacksmiths, belong to the Kammaalar caste. Divisions within the caste are by work. Among the carpenters *thachar aachaari* families still traditionally specialise in specific areas of temple, household, or agricultural carpentry. Within these groups the *sthapathis*, master craftsmen in house building, traditionally organised the carpenters and were responsible for the building ceremonies which were conducted according to the *Shaastraic* texts.

As patronage for traditional arts demanding fine detailing has disappeared, the number of craftsmen engaged in this art has also dropped sharply. Even during the last century, migration of craftsmen occurred in those areas where patronage was highest.Currently, in Tamilnadu, small concentrations of carpenters (50-400 families) exist in several areas such as Karaikudi, Kottaiyur, Devakottai, Madurai, Erode and Salem. Earlier, an area was distinguished by its speciality, such as the wood and glass work of Thanjavur, but many of the original specialities have been lost or diffused among several areas as craftsmen changed their styles to accommodate demand. The carpenter family is still a familiar adjunct to almost every village. Even here, the carpenter with the best skill acquires a wide reputation and draws clients from all the nearby areas.

Despite the antiquity of carpentry and woodcarving in Tamilnadu, very little has survived in wood from before the 18th century. Textual evidence, as well as evidence of woodcarving techniques duplicated in stone, point to a well- developed art of carving from the earliest documented times. The most visual evidence is the early stone monolithic *rathas* of the Pallavas of the seventh century in Mamallapuram, which systematically imitate in stone the wooden origins of their temple prototypes, including their carved beam endings and arched ceilings. Early temple icons were also traditionally in wood, and at least one possibly very early icon survives in a ruined Pallava temple at Kanchipuram today.

The early sixth century text, *Brihath Samhitha* by Varahamihira, known in Tamilnadu, describes all the attributes of wood and speaks of its sanctity, outlining the many types of indigenous trees and how one identifies auspicious trees, what wood is to be used in carving icons and in house building, and what ceremonies are to be performed in the process of using this wood. Tamil texts like the *Mayamatha* (circa 10th century) which was thought to have been used by the Cholas or the North Indian *Shilpa Shaastras* (circa 11th century) which also elaborate on the carpenter himself, all correspond to the *Brihath Samhitha* in their general treatment of wood.

Wooden temple art, which was earlier the height of Tamil woodcarving, is a dying art today. Its most eloquent survivor is the temple car (*ther*). These cars vary in size up to eight metres of intricate carving and consist of multiple set-in panels of a myriad deities, mythical animals like *yaalis* and *makaras*, real animals, *ganas*, dancers, erotic figures and decorative floral motifs. Detailed and stylised in high relief and occasionally very sensitively carved, the panels have their counterparts in the earlier stone and lime figures of nearby temples.

Wood craftsman

A carver at work on an intricate d[...]

Following page

Incarnations of Vishnu

Close-up of the side view of [...] car of the Varadaraajaswam[...] Kanchipuram, depicting the *av*[...] incarnations of Vishnu.

Like a huge *vimaana* suspended on four to eight massive wheels, the temple car serves as a shrine and platform for the temple deity. Height and colour are added by elaborate decorations of colourful cloth panels tied to a wooden structure surmounting the carved base. The temple car carries the *uthsavam* (festival) deity on the highest platform, crowned and bedecked with jewels and profusely garlanded with flowers. Accompanying the deity on the wooden base are a large painted wooden charioteer, two painted wooden guardians and two prancing white horses. Fully decorated, the car is pulled with thick ropes by devotees through the streets of the village or town during a special festival once a year.

This tradition is an ancient one. Although the earliest remaining cars are most likely datable to the 18th and 19th centuries, the tradition has well-established antecedents both in literature, inscriptions and in stone. By the 12th century, the later Chola temples in Melakkadambur and Darasuram were built as stone chariots on wheels. As with many of the temple concepts, these wooden chariots also may have developed out of the earlier symbolism of kingship embodied by the royal chariot as described in the early Tamil literature of the Sangam period. Today, these cars can be found at all major temples, and many exquisite ones still exist in the vicinity of older temples now languishing in small villages throughout Tamilnadu.

As with the temple car processions, several festivals occur throughout the year when the deity, profusely decorated with jewels and flowers and riding on his wooden-carved *vaahana*, is paraded through the streets. For example, during the ten days preceding the Tamil New Year (14 April) the deity is taken daily in procession, usually on the following mounts: *singam* (lion), *kaamadhenu* (winged cow), *annapakshi* (mythical bird), Ravana at Kailasa, *vimaana* (flying chariot), *vrishabham* (bull), horse, smaller temple car, *ratha* and the *pushpapalaka* (a type of open shrine). Besides all or some of these, a temple may also possess an elephant mount and a cobra mount. These wooden mounts are either painted or embossed with brass-plating, silver-plating or silver with gold. Generally, the plating is also undertaken by the carpenter.

Much wooden temple art, like its stone counter-

part, was painted. The traditional colours were blue, green, red, turmeric and white. The early technique of vegetable colouring and preparations used on the wood has, to a large extent, been lost. The 19th and early 20th century techniques of grinding cakes of colour to a fine powder which was mixed with a white lead primer and then strained through a cloth are still remembered, though not practised due to the lack of demand, lack of the mixture and the ease with which modern enamel paints can be applied. Thanjavur was a centre of excellence in this art during the 19th century.

Woodwork in Tamil houses, though limited in its application, has been a continued tradition and remains the major source of employment for carpenters. The average Hindu house of middle class and affluent Tamil families was traditionally built of brick and lime, with sloping wood and red tiled roofs. Each house had a raised veranda in front and at least one open courtyard in the interior. Detailing on woodwork was prevalent on the columns that supported the veranda and the sloping roof on the interior courtyard.

The front door was also given special attention as a sacred threshold and one or more carved panels representing Hindu deities and auspicious Hindu motifs like the *hamsa* (mythical swan), *padma* (lotus), *poornakumbha* (cornucopia), *kaamadhenu*, and patterned floral motifs crowned the door. The choice and combination of motifs as well as the style of carving and, in some cases, the type of wood used, varied from region to region and often from caste to caste. Geometrical motifs were rare. The amount of detailing in wood appears to have depended primarily on affluence, and in most rural homes very little ornamental woodwork in architecture is to be found.

Tamilnadu is, however, dotted throughout with the remains of elegant houses of merchants and zamindars and petty royalty dating from the mid-19th to the early 20th century. These houses display an ornateness in carving and detail lacking in less affluent homes. It is a tragedy that many of these houses have already been destroyed and that each year more of them are sold for their woodwork and subsequently demolished. Although the tradition of double-storeyed houses is described in the epic *Silappadikaaram*, nothing

Previous pages

Carved column, Chettinad

Wooden teak column with carved parrot capital supporting the wooden ceiling of a Naattukottai Chettiar house in Chettinad (circa 1890).

Wooden house, Karaikudi, Chettinad

An elaborately carved traditional door frame leading to the courtyard of a house in Karaikudi, Chettinad.

The opening is generally about 1.5 to 1.75 metres in height with a panel of deities carved above it, so that the person who passes through the entrance has to bend his head as an act of humility towards the deities.

Opposite page

Combs, Aanamalai Hills

Engraved bamboo combs used by the Kadar tribes of the Aanamalai Hills.

(Courtesy : Government Museum, Madras).

of the earlier opulence of architectural woodcraft has survived the hot, humid climate of Tamilnadu.

One striking exception is the exquisite wooden Padmanabhapuram palace in Kanyakumari district. Located in Tamilnadu, the palace was earlier the seat of the Travancore kings. Continuously enlarged over a 200-year period, the three-storeyed completely wooden inner palace is believed to date from the 17th century. The building plan which relies primarily on wood, even for its walls, the intricately carved roof gables, lathe-turned columns, carved window grills, decorated wooden ceilings and techniques of beaming and motifs, are particular to Kerala and specifically to Travancore.

In the vicinity of the Padmanabhapuram palace, there are several other wooden homes (*thara-vaad*), also in the Kerala style. These homes are characterised by their wooden walls, their systems of storage and their separate granary. The granary is a small, elegant, self-contained building located in front of the house with an arched open entrance which must be passed through to reach the main house. The architectural traditions of Kerala are prevalent in the thickly wooded bilingual Tamil-Malayalam border districts of Tamilnadu, such as Kanyakumari and Coimbatore. They disappear along with the intensive use of wood in house construction as the landscape becomes drier and less forested.

In the heart of Tamilnadu, the Nagarathaar Chettiars, wealthy merchants with business connections in Southeast Asia, became the patrons for much of the intricate architectural wood carving in the late 19th and 20th centuries. Their large, ornate homes, often reaching one city block in length, are concentrated in their 76 ancestral villages in Chettinad, comprising parts of Ramnad, Pudukottai and Thiruchirapalli districts. Wood carving was singularly important to the Chettiars, and they imported quantities of good Burmese teak for all their columns and doors. Several hundred families of carpenters migrated from Thirunelveli and the surrounding areas to Chettinad to meet the demand and, by the 20th century, Chettinad carpenters had become well-known for their skill and precision.

The houses are characterised primarily by massive doorways up to five metres in height, with in-

tricately carved panels of deities, often Gajalakshmi, or of the *Ramapattaabhishekam*, the coronation or marriage of Rama, above the door, and with intricate side panels of guardian soldiers on rearing horses, a motif popular even in stone under the Nayak kings of Madurai. Rows of delicate carvings of deer, *hamsa*, lotus, *rudraaksham* beads, and sometimes horses and floral motifs line the most ornate doors. The sanctity of each threshold is marked even within the house by a single panel of carved deities on all the interior doors. These are often short, only one and a half metres high. It was thought that a view of the deity over the door, and the act of bending to enter the door, would induce reverence and humility in the occupant and bring prosperity to the house.

Other wooden features of the Chettiar house are the rows of wooden columns with intricately carved capitals in stylised floral motifs, often set with parrots and occasionally with deities. The use of flattened circles to indicate patterns was common in the Ramnad area at the turn of the century. Later patterns, usually stylised floral motifs, were bolder and less intricate in their carving, but attractive in their proportions. These columns support the roofs of the outside veranda and the raised platforms used for seating at either end of the main courtyard. The slanting roof of the courtyard is supported either by a series of the same slightly more elongated wooden columns with wooden corbels, or more often by stone columns capped with wooden corbels. Unlike the northern *havelis*, Chettiar houses devote little attention to window detailing except for the occasional *yaali* carvings on the struts supporting the roof overhang or the window shades.

Further decoration in the homes was confined to paintings on ceilings and upper parts of walls and windows, imported tiling, and elaborate figures made of a lime, sand and jaggery mixture which decorated the exterior facade and gate. Furniture was uncommon in the Tamilnadu home as seating was on raised platforms. Decorative furniture items were the baby cot, (a British-influenced item in affluent Hindu homes), child-walker, trunks, cupboards, and low boxes for cash used in stores and business houses.

Ceremonial wooden items were common in wealthy homes. These consisted of small shrines for the *pooja* rooms, low carved stools for mar-

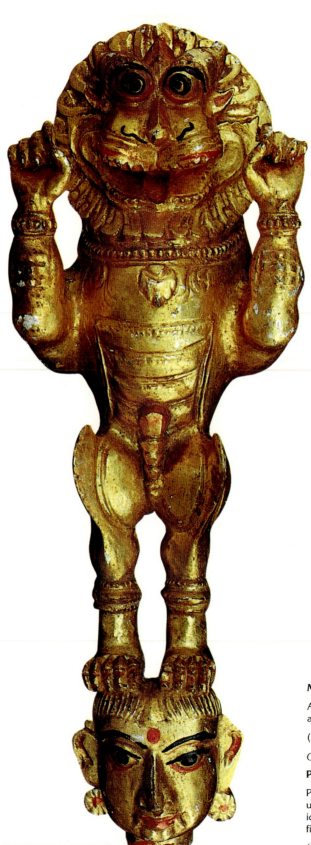

Mythical lion, wood

A *yaali* or mythical lion standing on a woman's head, painted with gold foil.

(Courtesy : Aparna Art Gallery, Madras).

Opposite page

Processional horse

Prancing white polychrome horse usually used as mount (*vaahana*) for an *uthsavam* idol in procession. Similar horses are also fixed on to the large temple cars.

(Courtesy : Aparna Art Gallery, Madras)

riages, carved fans for the deity, small wooden deities, fertility couples, and various small ceremonial containers. Special wooden carved panels of deities, or symbols of the deity fixed to either end of a metre-long pole, were other important ceremonial items. These panels (*kaavadi*) are carried even today on the shoulders of a person to fulfil a vow to Murugan, or Karthikeya. Intricately carved wooden kitchen instruments, such as grinders, vegetable cutters and serving ladle holders, given as part of a large dowry at marriage, and smaller objects like carved wooden covers for manuscripts, spices and *kumkum* boxes, games and some toys like wooden dolls and elephants also exhibit the range of skills of the carpenter.

In the late 19th century, the British attempted to revive craft skills for their export potential. Training courses for carpenters were organised in Tamilnadu, primarily in Madras at the Government College for Arts and Crafts. During this period, carved screens, picture frames, easels, jewellery chests, and furniture of heavy English Victorian style such as cabinets, desks, chairs, tables, and sideboards were produced primarily in Burmese teak and rosewood, and decorated with Hindu and floral motifs. These were used primarily by the British, wealthy merchants and royalty.

Although the tools used in the 1980s are the same crude implements of centuries ago, carpentry is one of the few craft areas which has kept pace with a changing market. Carpenters, whose fathers and grandfathers practised rites sanctifying their work and were often called to give intricate detailing, are now mainly employed in manufacturing utilitarian items such as doors, windows and simple furniture or agricultural implements. Except for a few areas like Kanyakumari, where the local carpenter still supplies his bullock carts with the traditional carved lotus panel, most woodcraft is plain. The families still practising carving and temple work are very few. Major carving today consists of panels of deities and free-standing figures and animals such as horses, which are given an antique painted look, primarily for the export market. These figures have their inspiration in the temple car panels and *vaahanas*.

Although the majority of carpenters have

dropped out of school early to start practising their craft, others have pursued their studies, and taken government training in the hope of getting regular long-term carpentry jobs. These same carpenters, if they belong to the Kammaalar caste, still trace their beginnings to Vishwakarma, the Creator, and many still celebrate the annual Ravana festival peculiar to their caste. At this festival, it is said that, after Sri Lanka had burned, Vishwakarma commanded the Kammaalars to take up their tools and rebuild the kingdom.

With the important role played by music and dance in the cultural life of Tamilnadu, it is inevitable that the making of musical instruments should become a major craft. Most of the centres of this craft are situated around Thanjavur, which has also produced some of the country's greatest musicians.

The Tamils classify their instruments not only according to their types, but also according to the different occasions on which they are used. The *naadaswaram* is an essential part of the marriage ceremony and the *kombu* is associated with religious festivities. Percussion instruments are sometimes used to make announcements, just as the tomtoms in Africa are used to pass on messages from one village to another. They announce the auspicious procession of village deities, as well as funeral processions of certain castes. In the past, general proclamations made by the king were announced to the beat of drums, a practice known as *thandora*.

The *Silappadikaaram* mentions the *yaazh*, an ancient Tamil instrument similar to the harp or lute. Though obsolete now, it occupied a prominent place in the world of music in ancient times, and references to it abound in the Tamil classics. There were several types of *yaazh*, from the simple curved bamboo bow to elaborately carved wooden instruments in the shape of crocodiles, boats, fishes, and so on.

With the advent of the *veena*, the various types of *yaazh* which were capable of emitting only a single note were relegated to the background. Unlike the *yaazh* with its limited scope, the *veena* is capable of producing a wide range of sounds. Made of jackwood, the various parts of the *veena*, namely the *kudam* (pot), top plank, neck, and *yaali* (which represents a lion's face) are first assembled and a mixture of honeywax and black

powder is applied to the top plank. The bridge is then set on level and the position of the frets, 24 in number, is determined according to the *swarasthaanam*, which literally means 'place of *swaras*' (the notes). The frets, the bridge and the side-plate are all made of brass. Thanjavur is a renowned centre for the manufacture of *veenas* and the families employed in making the instrument have been following the traditions set by their forefathers. It takes about ten days for a craftsman to complete a single *veena*.

Essentially used to keep *shruthi*, which may be loosely defined as 'musical tone', the *thamburaa* is similar in manufacture and appearance to the *veena* but for the *yaali* face and the neck which are absent here. The Tamil *thamburaa* has a wooden base, unlike the north Indian instrument which has a base made of a marrow.

The wood used for making musical instruments undergoes an elaborate process of seasoning. In the *veena*, the *thamburaa* and the *gottu vaadyam* (similar to the veena but without the frets), the wood used for the bowl and trunk is scooped out from a single block.

The *morsing* is in the shape of an elongated triangle, with a small steel wire joining two ends. It is made of iron and steel, and is moulded into shape.

The flute, known as the *kuzhal* in Tamil, is a wind instrument associated with Lord Krishna. The general term given for this is *vangiyam*. The *vangiya vaadyams* made of bamboo, sandalwood, bronze, *sengaali* and *karungaali* (types of wood). The bamboo is first dried in the sun and then baked in fire and seasoned. The holes, 12 in number, are gouged out of the length of the bamboo and are placed at definite intervals, based on the *swarasthaanam*. The flute is generally made to order, since it is normally not as much in demand as, say, the stringed instruments. Tribes, such as the Kadars and Todas, have their own simple varieties of bamboo flutes.

The *naadaswaram* is another wind insturment, made of *aachamaram*, a species of wood. *Naadaswaram*-playing was initially confined to the families of barbers, and even now only these families are employed in the making of the instrument, which plays an important role in temple festivities. A unique feature of the Thiruvarur tem-

Opposite page

Religious panel, detail

A detail of a wooden panel of Kaliyamardhana Krishna showing details of workmanship. The wood used is generally country wood.

(Courtesy : Rani Arts and Crafts, Madras)

Wood carving of the *hamsa*

Wood carving was and still is a widely-practised art, used to decorate parts of the house such as doors, windows and pillars, or the chariots used in temple festivals. Perfection of form and intricacy of detail are as important as the finished form. The *hamsa* or mythical swan is a very popular motif in Tamilnadu, be it carved on a temple or a chariot or woven into a sari.

ple in Thanjavur District is the *naadaswaram* made out of soapstone which is played every day during the *pooja*.

Ancient Tamilnadu appears to have specialised in drums. A large number of kettle drums, double-headed drums, earthenware drums, one-headed drums, tambourines, tabors and tapering drums are listed in Tamil literary works. They were instruments which provided musical accompaniment. Different kinds of raw materials were used for manufacturing the *muzhavu-vaadyas* (percussion instruments) like *kanjam, karungaali* wood, *sengaali* wood, *vempal, palaa* and *kuramaram*.

Among the best known and most commonly used drums is the *mridangam*, which is shaped like a barrel. The two mouth-ends are covered with buffalo-hide, drawn taut with the help of leather thongs. The sides of a log of wood, generally jackwood, are sawed off, then turned on a hand lathe. The *thavil*, made of jackwood, also employs the process of turning. Like the *mridangam*, this is a circular barrel with buffalo-hide drawn taut on either end. The *ganjiraa* is a circular piece of jackwood, scooped out and covered with the skin of the *udumbu*, a type of giant lizard, with a few coins around its circumference to provide additional music.

Manamadurai in Ramnad District is the only place where mud is available in the requisite consistency for the making of the *ghatam*, which is similar in shape to a pot. The *shruthi* is determined according to the thickness of the walls of the pot.

The *panchamukhavaadyam* or the five-faced percussion instrument is unique. As its name implies, it is made up of five small drum-like structures welded on to a similar but larger sized structure, highly decorated with engravings of the *yaali* and floral patterns, with a narrow bottom made of brass and copper. There are also two brass *kudams* or pots alongside, the mouths of which are secured tightly with cow-hide; together, the instrument is known as the *panchamukhavaadyam* with *kudamuzhaa*. An important ritual of the Thiruvarur temple is the playing of this unique instrument at its *moonru kaala pooja*, which is performed in the morning, at noon and in the evening.

Ancient wooden musical instrument

Makara yaazh, a harp-like string instrument in the form of a crocodile, carved out of wood. The *yaazh* was developed from the simple bow. It is referred to in the Tamil Sangam literature but is not used nowadays.

(Courtesy : Development Centre for Musical Instruments, Madras)

Opposite page, top

A *mridangam* maker at work

Leather thongs are stretched tight over the long barrelshaped body.

Opposite page, bottom

Tuning a *veena*

The foremost of the folk instruments can be said to be the *villadi vaadyam*. This consists of an enormous mud pot, like the *ghatam*, to the neck of which is attached a long strip of bamboo, on to which are attached, at intervals, small round brass bells. The instrument is played with a table tennis racquet-like instrument made of cow-hide, which is beaten against the mouth of the pot, while the other hand shakes the cane with the bells on it.

Among other important temple instruments are the *surya pirai* percussion instruments made of thin parchment; the *kombu* or horn, used during temple festivities and in martial music ; the *gowrikalam*, a wind instrument made of brass tubes fitted to each other; and the *udukkai*, a drum shaped like an hourglass, with a shell of brass, wood or clay, laced with twine and used for exorcism. The list of instruments is endless, each with its unique construction and function but made of either hide or jackwood.

Hallowed by its association with Vishnu, the conch or *sangu* is used in temples, and during religious ceremonies and processions. It is the most ancient wind instrument known to man. Blown through a small hole made in the spiral, the conch is elaborately decorated with metal engravings which cover it and elongate the shell.

The materials used in the manufacture of musical instruments and their accessories are jackwood (preferred for its quality of *naadam* or tone), blackwood, redwood, ivory, *rakta chandana*, *kadira* wood, ebony, silver oak, pine, Himalayan fir, red and white cedar, margosa, gourd, bamboo, cane, reed, earthenware, the skin of sheep, calf, and buffalo, and metals like silver, bronze, copper, and iron. Strings are made of gut, metal, silk and seasoned plant fibres. In very ancient times, the strings were made of *darbha* grass, properly seasoned and twisted.

Once upon a time, it is said, even stones were chiselled and polished till they were fit to be tapped for music in the temples of Tamilnadu. Supporting this belief are the *sapthaswara thoon* or the seven-note musical pillars of the Meenakshi Amman Temple at Madurai, which produce a beautiful resonance when struck — a permanent monument to the Tamilian's involvement in music.

After the great megaliths of Tamilnadu, there is a period of total darkness in stone sculpture and architecture. Emerging in the sixth century AD is the rule of the Pallavas, with the rock-cut caves of Mamallapuram, its stone *rathas* (chariots) and stone shore temples, and the structural stone temples of Kanchipuram. Of all these, the greatest is "The Descent of the Ganga", a monolithic fresco of carvings, depicting the vivacity of life beside the discipline of Arjuna's penance. The style of the Pallava sculpture shows kinship with that of the Chalukyas of Aihole, Badami, and Pattadakkal, and it is reasonable to suppose that related guilds of *shilpis* produced the sculptures of the two kingdoms. Apart from granite, there are a few sandstone temples in the state, but sandstone as a medium was hardly favoured in Tamilnadu where granite is easily available.

The early Pandyas drew inspiration from the Pallavas.Their contribution was in the varied sculptural and iconographic forms, some of which were introduced to Tamilnadu for the first time. Apart from the numerous cave temples at Pillaiyarpatti, Aanamalai and Sittannavasal (better-known for its paintings), the unfinished sculptures of the monolithic rock at Vettuvankovil at Kalugumalai are notable for their power and elegance.

But the greatest stone temples and carvings appeared in the Chola period. The massive Brihadeeshvara temple at Thanjavur, with its profusion of carvings; the gentler, more elegant temple at Gangaikondacholapuram; the Airavatheshavara temple at Darasuram; and the Kampahareshvara temple at Thribhuvanam are a few examples of what the Chola craftsmen could achieve. Engineering skill, demonstrated in the lifting of the massive cupola on to the top of the *vimaana* in Thanjavur, combined with the chiseller's art, were required to create these granite wonders. The sculptures of Shiva and the *karanas* or poses of Bharatha Natyam reflect the Chola Kings religious and artistic inclinations. The Nataraja and Chandesaanugrahamurthi of Gangaikondacholapuram are as forceful as the Chola bronzes, immortalising a moment in time. The Darasuram *ratha* gave birth to a rash of chariot-shaped stone temples which culminated in the sun temple of Konarak in Orissa, influenced by the Chola conquerors of the east.

The Chola temples are the finest examples of the Dravida (southern) school of architecture. By this time, the role of the temple as the socio-economic nucleus of town life had been firmly established, and large complexes with *praakaaras* (circumambulatory passages), *mandapas* (pillared halls), and Devi shrines were introduced.

Several temples of Tamilnadu have outstanding features because of which the state is often referred to as "the land of temples". Chidambaram has beautiful panels depicting the 108 *karanas* of the *Natya Shaastra* (the canon of dance), as performed by women. Its various *sabhas* or halls are intended to inspire awe. Kanchipuram is the city of temples, starting from the earliest Pallava times down to the Nayak period and even later. If the Ekambareshwara temple is grand, the Varadaraaja temple has some noteworthy features, such as an exquisite monolithic stone chain. But the most famous of the temples is that of Meenakshi at Madurai, with its profusion of sculptures and magnificent proportions, the thousand-pillared *mandapas* and the pillars of stone, its towering *gopurams* and larger-than-life-sized reliefs. Madurai is the pinnacle of the stone sculptor's skill, if not his artistry. The skill continues elsewhere, as in the long corridor of the Rameshwaram temple, and it is a skill which continues till the present day.

Mahishasuramardhini, Mamallapuram, Pallava, 7th century, AD.

The fiery war between Durga and the buffalo demon is seen in this dynamic wall panel inside a cave. The eight-armed goddess and her lion *vaahana* are attacking an enormous Mahisha.

Milkman and cattle, Govardhana cave, Mamallapuram, Pallava, 7th century AD

In sharp contrast to the fiery Durga, this charming scene of the cow lovingly licking her calf shows the range of emotions that the stone sculptors were able to depict.

Today, granite carving is confined to the area around Mamallapuram and Chingleput, probably because of the existence of the Mamallapuram School of Sculpture set up by the government. As in bronze, 20th century sculpture has not yet evolved an idiom of its own, and many of the carvings are copies of earlier periods. However, a few sculptors have made a mark, and their work adorns temples all over the world.

Granite images are essential for the construction of the *sthirabera* or the fixed consecrated icons. Today this sculpture is concentrated around Mamallapuram, where artisans chisel away at granite blocks to produce massive pillars as well as small icons. There are also a few pockets elsewhere in the state, where stone carving is practised.

The sculptors belong to the Vishwakarma or Kammaalar community. From this community come the stone artists, woodworkers, temple planners, jewellers and metal craftsmen. In Tamilnadu, *shilpis* live chiefly in Thirunelveli, Ramnad, Madurai, Chinglepet and North Arcot districts. Since it has no stone, Thanjavur has mainly metal craftsmen.

The quality of the material is an extremely important part of the sculptural process. Just as the *Shilpa Shaastras* set out the measurements and techniques of sculpting, they have also gone into great detail regarding the quality of stone, its maturity, texture, colour and so on.

The details and great delicacy of rendering require that the stone used in sculpture remains hard, without losing its shape or chipping off unexpectedly. The stability and durability of the final form depends a great deal on the homogeneity of the stone. For this reason, the traditional artists work with the indigenous varieties available in the state, as it is extremely durable for construction purposes. The stones have to be selected carefully for their texture and for the lie of the stone (or the direction of growth). This lie also defines the quarrying technique employed. Where stone for sculpture is concerned, dynamiting of rocks is not recommended since cracks would be formed. The stone is cut by moving a series of wedges about 5 to 7.5 cm deep. These wedges are driven in carefully with heavy 4 kg hammers, resulting in the rocks breaking apart with clean

Gayathri, Meenakshi temple, Madurai, Nayak, 17th century

Gayathri is the wife of Brahma, symbolic of earth, ether and the heavens, the subject of the most sacred of all prayers, the *Gayathri manthram*. Nayak sculpture makes up in elaborately carved detail what it lacks in emotional content which is so strong in Pallava and Chola art.

Gopuram and *vimaana*, **Meenakshi temple, Madurai, Nayak, 17th century.**

Madurai was the ancient capital of the Pandya rulers of Tamilnadu. The Sangams, ancient Tamil conferences to promote language and literature, were held here. The gradual growth of the temple complex over the years has resulted in a bewildering maze of *mandapas*, subsidiary shrines, storerooms, *yagna* halls, kitchens, and so on. The four *gopurams* or gateways are massive and dwarf the main *vimaana* with its gold-plated *shikhara*. The temple is notable for its profusion of sculptures rich, baroque and colourful.

edges. Till recently, even the quarry workmen belonged to the artist-craftsmen community and hence the art was a continuous process from material sizing to the finished pieces.

Good stone should also have no flaws, namely *kalanga* or stain, *rekha* or patch, and *bindu* or spot. The sculptural masterpieces created in Mamallapuram are not of the best variety of stone. But, since the task there was not to create images for worship but for aesthetic purposes, the secondary nature of the stone was considered acceptable.

The tools used by stone sculptors are made of mild steel in various sizes. They are the hammer and the chisel, the main tools of sculptors even today. The action of the sculptor is to peck out the stone, and not cut it. To prevent it from cracking due to the vibration of the instrument, the image is always carved when the stone is laid flat on the ground, irrespective of its seated or standing posture.

Unlike other materials, stone has some inherent lacunae. Metal is capable of adopting daring form and the clear outlines it defines give dramatic shadow and light effects. Wood can be carved with almost unlimited complexity and hence produces an impression of elaboration and lightness. Stone, on the other hand, needs to be handled with care. To make the stone more rigid, the artist uses metal holdfasts to link unsupported limbs while working, and later removes them.

The themes for most of the sculptures have always been religious in nature. Much of the elaboration has a strong basis in the mythology and Puraanic tradition of India. There is an elaborate use of symbolism to convey the meaning of abstract intangible truths.

The artist uses dance and Yoga postures a great deal to heighten the effect of the composition. This lends both grace and movement to a frozen art form. Above all, the expression on the face of the image is held to be the most important part of the sculpture. Where images for worship are concerned, the face is carefully carved to evoke a feeling of tranquillity, reverence, and love in the heart of the devotee. After the completion of a sculptural piece, a ceremony known as *nayanon-*

Lingodbhava, Brihadeeshvara temple, Thanjavur, Chola, 10th century AD

In this form Shiva himself emerges from the *linga* to tell Brahma and Vishnu that the *linga* has no top or bottom, and that they too were born of his loins.

**The coronation of Vibheeshana,
Ramaswami temple, Kumbakonam, Nayak,
17th century**

The temple illustrates the various episodes of
the *Ramayana*. In this panel, Rama performs
the *raajyaabhishekham* of Vibheeshana,
brother of the *raakshasa* ruler of Lanka,
Ravana. Nayak sculpture, following the
Vijayanagara style, is baroque and exquisite
in its depiction of detail.

A *sthapathi* at work

Enormous granite blocks are sculpted by hand with a chisel and hammer. The same methods used to create the monolithic Pallava structures are still used today.

(Courtesy : College of Architecture and Sculpture, Mamallapuram).

Opposite page

Wheel and horses, Darasuram, Chola, 12th century, AD

The temple is a Chola masterpiece, built in the form of a chariot. With exquisite carvings of gods and goddesses, it stresses the themes of dance and music. The *mandapa* is the dance theatre and the temple emphasises the importance of the fine arts under the Cholas.

Soapstone or _maakal_ figure of Ganesha

As these are much cheaper than granite, they are popular images for the domestic _pooja_.

Opposite page

Kalchutti, **soapstone utensil**

Soapstone is a favourite medium for cooking, particularly items made of tamarind which is a common ingredient in Tamil cooking.

milan is conducted, wherein the image is invested with sight, life and breath, thus becoming a virtual living force. And only then is the image ceremoniously placed in the *garbhagriha* or sanctum sanctorum.

A subsidiary form of carving is soapstone or *maakal* carving, found in the region between Pondicherry and Cuddalore and around Salem. An easy material to manipulate, soapstone does not achieve the sensitivity of granite. It is primarily the material used to create the lathe-turned stoneware utensils, known as *kalchutti*, used for making tamarind and lime-based dishes, particularly the *kozhambus* and buttermilk of Tamil cuisine. In recent times, the exorbitant prices of granite carvings have made the soapstone figures of deities extremely competitive and popular. These figures are sold around places of pilgrimage and tourist centres, catering to a moving population. They are generally small, about half a metre in height and, along with metal images, are kept in the family *pooja* room. Soapstone is very pliable—it can be cut with a handsaw and chiselled with simple tools. But it is this very pliability which makes it incapable of producing the emotional undertones of the harder granite.

Translated from Tamil by Nanditha Krishna with assistance from Shashikala.

Thanjavur Paintings

The turbulent conditions that existed in northern India during the Middle Ages resulted in an exodus of artists and poets to the south, and the Vijayanagara kingdom fostered a great burgeoning of the arts, particularly of paintings. The Vijayanagara artist was responsible for the development of three distinct schools of art — the Deccani School, the Mysore School and the Thanjavur School. The Mysore School reached its zenith during the rule of Mummadi Krishnaraja Wodeyar in the 18th century, while in Thanjavur the Maratha kings developed a distinct style of painting. The credit for the development and establishment of this ornate style of "Tanjore Paintings", as they are known, goes to Serfoji Maharaja of Thanjavur.

The paintings are characterised by the use of primary colours, generally avoiding mixtures, with stylised modelling effects by shading the inside of the contours. Jewels, drapery and architectural elements like pillars and canopies are slightly raised as in low relief by the use of a special plaster, covered with pure gold-leaf and embedded with semi-precious stones in different hues.

Sometimes gold-coated silver-leaf was used. Colourful glass pieces and occasionally pearls were used to embellish the Thanjavur painting, which feature gave it an edge over the Mysore painting. The painter himself procured the colours, which were prepared along the lines described in ancient texts. Besides minerals, he used the leaves and flowers of certain plants. In modern times, waterproof plywood, which has the advantage of being available in any size, is used. Thick brown paper or thin cardboard is pasted, utilising *maida* (flour) or tamarind seed paste as an adhesive. The paper is fixed on the wooden plank with the help of a rich paste of the required thickness. Over this paste, unbleached long cloth or mull is spread smoothly, avoiding wrinkles. This surface is then coated with a combination of gum Arabic, French chalk powder, copper sulphate and a little *gopi* (yellow powder). Thus treated, the surface is later played with a rounded glass, usually a paper-weight or a bottle. To obtain the best results, the surface has to be absolutely smooth. Formerly, sketching charcoal was obtained from straight twigs of the tamarind tree, which were cut to a suitable size and placed on a heated iron table. The charred twigs were then used as sketching charcoal.

Colours of mineral origin were reduced to powder in a mortar and, after being soaked in water for several hours, were made into a fine paste before being applied. When primary colours were mixed, they were ground in the mortar for proper blending, to obtain the distinct colours needed. Brushes for painting were generally made of squirrel's hair. These were needed for delicate work. For drawing superfine lines, brushes made of the pointed blade of a special variety of grass had to be used. Today, these conventional stipulations are, however, dispensed with, if easier and equally effective alternatives are available.

A rough sketch of the picture is drawn with a crayon. For pictures of larger proportions, if a copy of the standard picture is available, a perforated stencil is used to draw the outline. The next step is to draw the sketch and then paint the farthest objects such as the sky or river. The animal and human figures, their dress and ornaments, need greater attention, and here the taste and the choice of the painter generally reveal his artistic inclinations. It is the degree of embellishment that is the distinguishing feature of a Thanjavur painting. Hence the importance of the gesso work or gold-covering of portions of jewellery. The gold work is generally taken up in the morning, when the picture and base of the gold-foil is moist, so as to hold the foil firmly. When the foil extends beyond the required margin, colour is used to cover it; then the gold-covered portions are outlined in black. Once the paint is dry and the finishing touches are complete, it is glazed. The painting now looks resplendent because of the use of gold and the richness of the colours.

The Thanjavur artist does not regard a portrait as a study of character — the individuality of the subject is identified to a lesser extent than the general decorative effect. In these paintings the figures are depicted in proportion to their importance; the principal figure therefore is always on a larger scale than the rest. Representations of deities under ornate canopies with finely-executed pillars, draperies folded in gentle scallops, garlands of ropes, chandeliers, cushions and furniture, all lend an aura of opulence. The dark-hued Lord Krishna is sometimes depicted as a fair cherub, indicating European influence.

Thanjavur paintings date from the middle of the 18th to the middle of the 19th century. They were painted on wood, glass, mica, ivory, and on walls. With the advent of British rule, Englishmen at the king's court and musicians playing different instruments were painted along with the main subject. Because the painters were Vaishnavites, the subjects were usually Rama, Krishna, Lakshmi, Narasimha, and so on. But the Shaivites introduced Uma Maheshwara, Ganesha, Nataraja, Murugan, Meenakshi, Parvati and other Shaivite deities.

This style of painting slowly disappeared because of the time involved and the prohibitive cost. But in recent times there is a definite revival and Thanjavur paintings are once again becoming very popular. Even today, there are a few families belonging to the original Raju clan living in Thanjavur, Srirangam and Kumbakonam who carry on this traditional art.

Apart from the gem and gold-leaf encrusted paintings of Thanjavur, there is a separate — though undoubtedly related — tradition of painting on glass, mica, and ivory which was introduced around the 18th century. The glass paintings, in particular, constituted a difficult genre, as the sequence of steps had to be reversed to achieve the desired result. Thus, after the picture was drawn, it was shaded in first and then decorated with gold-leaf, a process that resulted in a

Opposite page, top

Process

The making of a Thanjavur painting, left to right : First paper and white mull are pasted over a plywood sheet, then coated with a mixture of gum Arabic, French chalk powder, copper sulphate and *gopi*. The picture is then drawn— charred twigs were formerly used, now substituted by pencil. The gold-leaf covering then begins, with a black outline to conceal uneven edges.

Opposite page, bottom

S. Kuppuswamy Raja, master craftsman and descendant of a well-known family of Thanjavur painters, adds the finishing touches

***Pattabhi Rama**, or the coronation of Lord Rama*

The artists used basic colours and shading was virtually unknown. The strong European influence can be seen in the draperies and the winged angels hovering above.

(Courtesy : V.R. Govindarajan)

Krishna, glass painting

These paintings appeared in the 18th century through Chinese influence. They are used in the *pooja* and are still worshipped in Tamilian houses

(Courtesy : Aparna Art Gallery)

Details on p. 136 and 137

Balakrishna, the child Krishna, a popular subject in Thanjavur paintings

Unlike the normally blue portraits of Krishna, he is always painted white in this School of Art. The figures are rotund and cherubic, the main subject enlarged out of proportion to the others. A repoussé effect is created by gold-leaf gésso work studded with pearls, glass, and semi-precious stones.

(Courtesy : V.K.Rajamani)

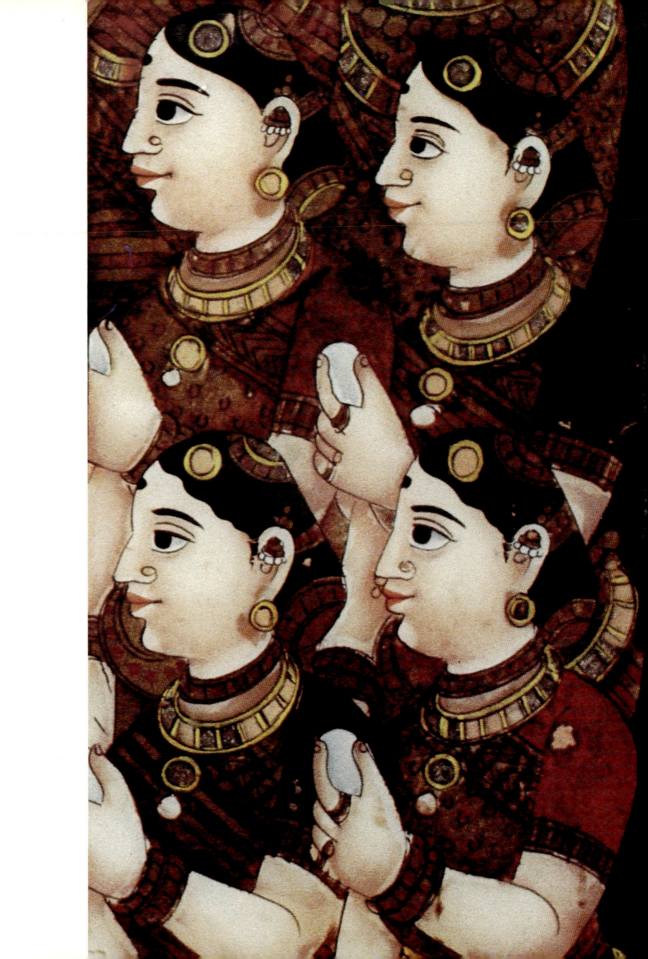

Gajalakshmi glass painting

This picture of the goddess— happy, cherubic and cheerful — became so popular that it became symbolic of auspiciousness itself.

(Courtesy : Aparna Art Gallery)

Opposite page

Secular painting

Secular subjects were popular in glass paintings, although their treatment was stiff and unnatural in the style of European portraiture. As the sequence of steps in painting was reversed (i.e. the shading came first, outlining last), a flat single-dimensional quality emerged.

(Courtesy : Madras Museum).

flat, single-dimensional effect, with doll-like figures. But the painting has the vital quality of folk art, which is its major redeeming feature. There is a remarkable directness of expression, and the message and symbolism are unerring.

It is believed that a group of Chinese artists lived and worked for many of the rulers and merchants whom they painted, and glass paintings are believed to have been introduced into India as a result of Chinese influence. The themes of glass paintings were religious or depictions of women or portraits of patrons. The religious paintings are highly decorative and flat, and the paintings of women heavily stylised. It is in the execution of portraits that an effort was made to infuse reality, to compliment the subjects of the artist's work. There is a dignity and even gentleness in treating these subjects. The British influence is evident in the Victorian architecture of the background, the furniture and even the oval format.

Tha fact that religious themes were ideal for the *pooja* made them instantly popular, and most traditional homes in Tamilnadu still contain glass paintings which are an integral part of the family prayer room.

Basketry & Fibre Craft

The villages of Tamilnadu are dotted with palm trees coconut, date, and palmyra — and over the centuries the palm has become a major source of raw material for basketry and related products. Bamboo, cane, grasses, fibres and reeds are also used in the making of baskets, thatch, ropes, mats and many other things, since these are the cheapest and most easily available natural materials.

Though basketry is practised throughout the state, only a few centres are engaged in mass production and trading. Concentrations of workers are to be found in Dharmapuri, Salem, Coimbatore, South Arcot and Thiruchirapalli districts.

Tamilnadu farmers depend mainly on bamboo baskets to store and carry foodgrains, in which case the inner and outer surfaces of the baskets are covered with cow-dung. These baskets are also used for packing and transporting fruits and flowers. Bamboo is generally considered a delicate wood, to be carefully utilised.

Cane, which is sturdier, goes chiefly into the making of furniture, bowls, and other items of household use. These are made in Madras, North Arcot and Thanjavur districts. An even sturdier material is the stem of the forest plant called *azhingi*, from which baskets are fashioned. Because the material is extremely strong and can withstand rough handling, these baskets are employed in the construction trade to carry bricks, mortar and mud.

Baskets are also made out of palmyra fibres and leaves which are braided in various patterns, each named after a fruit, vegetable or flower. The stem of the date palm provides baskets very similar to the bamboo products used in homes.

Like basketry, mat-weaving is a very ancient craft and is carried on throughout Tamilnadu. Regarded as the common man's bed, mats of exquisite design and quality are made from various types of grass, seeds, and leaves, including those of the screw pine and the date and coconut palm. These mats, usually of the coarse variety in counts ranging from 16 to 26, are manufactured in the districts of North and South Arcot, Salem, Thiruchirapalli and Thanjavur. The medium coarse variety, ranging from 30 to 50 counts, is produced in Thirunelveli district.

But Pathamadai, a village in this district, produces a far finer variety of mats, with counts that range between 100 and 140. The famous Pathamadai mats are made from *korai* grass, which grows in abundance along the banks of rivers and in marshy places. It is said that the best mats come only from the wild variety of *korai*. The grass is collected from the marshes twice a year — in September/October and February/March. Then, sitting in the rain where the grass is still damp and soft, the mat weaver slices it into very fine threads, as thin as a human hair.

While the weft in the Pathamadai mats is of reed, the warp is of cotton or silk, depending upon the quality required. This warp consists usually of quadruple twisted 100-count yarn, that is, four strands of the 100-count yarn are taken hold of at one end and twisted on a *charkha* to produce a single thread of great strength. The warp is thus prepared by the men, but the actual weaving is done by the women. They sit upon a wooden bench with the warp threads stretched below them and a bamboo tripod carrying the reed in front. Explaining the weaving process, V. Natarajan writes: "A single grass is taken and dipped in a cup of water. One end of this wet grass is inserted in a hole of a long fine stick, which can be compared to a gigantic needle.

With the help of this stick the grass is passed into the loom. Afterwards the stick is removed and the grass is held on both sides by both hands and slightly twisted to give uniform roundness and strength. Then the reed is pressed against it several times to keep it in position. A woman can weave about 15 cm of 100 count or about 7.5 cm of 140 count per day."

After the weaving is complete, the mat is compressed to eliminate any unevenness, a process that takes between two to four hours. Thus, the weaver needs nearly 12 days to finish a single 100-count mat and up to 22 days for one of 140 counts. In comparison, most mats made in India use coarse yarn and can be turned out at the rate of two or three a day. The best Pathamadai mats weigh only 400 grams and are so pliable that they can easily be folded without causing any damage.

The mats are either in their natural single colour or combined in bands and stripes with the traditional red, green and black. Speaking of these mats, Kamaladevi Chattopadhyay observes : "The ivory-white mat, simple with no trace of design, is a superb piece, for its very simplicity has an allure all its own, with its soft liquid surface. The design called *malaikulam* has sqaures in the centre in various colours, then geometrical designs, and the border is left plain white. The design *gopuram* (temple tower) has only two colours, the natural and green with the towering roof in the centre ... The old patterns consist mainly of stripes, usually at the two ends, or little streaks through the body. In fact, these bring out the beauty of the texture more effectively."

In the days gone by, the mats were coloured with vegetable dyes from such plants as *sappaangu kattai*. The finely-powdered dried bark and leaves were sprinkled over the split *korai* grass, which would then be folded and soaked in salt water. The vessel was allowed to stand in the sun for about ten days until the grass was uniformly dyed. Today the large-scale use of synthetic dyes gives the artisans a range of many colours.

There is an interesting history behind the fine-quality Pathamadai mats. Their development is attributed to one Hassan Bawa Labbai, who lived about a century ago and whose forefathers were

Opposite page

Kolam reed

To produce a continuous design or *kolam*, hollow reeds are punctured with holes to form a design. The reed is filled with rice flour and rolled continuously to form a design on the floor. These are sold during temple festivals and are very popular at pilgrimage centres.

Palm leaf fan

The heat of Tamilnadu makes it essential for people to keep these fans around.

engaged in making coarse mats. It is said that Hassan was once drying *korai* grass in the sun, when there was a downpour accompanied by squally winds. His *korai* grass was blown off into the river. After the rain had stopped he salvaged the thoroughly-soaked grass and found, to his surprise, that it was soft and smooth. He discovered also that he could split the *korai* into strands of great fineness — hitherto he had been able to obtain counts of 30 to 40, but now he had before him strands of 100 to 200. So he commenced weaving with these strands. The mat he produced was of such softness that he repeated the process of soaking the grass in the river and then splitting it. From that time onwards, out of his looms flowed mats of exquisite quality. Soon his fellow artisans discovered his secret, and today the Labhai community of Pathamadai produces superb mats, which stand unsurpassed and unrivalled in the country.

Apart from the *korai* grass mats, Tamilnadu also produces mats made from the screw pine, date palm and palmyra leaf. These are used to pack *jaggery,* tamarind and other agricultural produce. The coconut leaf mats, which provide thatch for roofs, are made in almost every village in the state. Used to erect temporary sheds or pandals, they can be built in elaborate architectural shapes on ceremonial occasions.

In several areas of Tamilnadu, the palmyra leaf is transformed into a great many utility items, marked with high imagination and fine skill. These include fruit trays, picnic baskets, shopping bags, handbags, screens, *chiks* and glass-holders. Ramanathapuram district is famous for its beautiful sieves and winnows, while Daripatnam specialises in hand fans and square mats. Best known, perhaps, is Rameshwaram for its highly decorative square baskets with their raised patterns, which make excellent trinket boxes. A wide range of toys is produced, including animals, birds and rattles.

Fibre craft too has been developed among the women of Tamilnadu, particularly in Kanyakumari district. Using banana, sisal, aloe, screw pine and pineapple fibre, the women turn out table mats and many kinds of bags.

A variation of reeds and fibres is pith, which is used to make models of temples and dynamic

Child's rattle made of palm leaf

Opposite page , left

Colourfully-dyed palm leaf *moram* **or de-husking tray, Thirunelveli**

Opposite page , right

Palm leaf baskets, Chettinad, famous for the square effect of their weave

Opposite page, bottom

Container

An old *vetrilaipaakku petti* (or *chellapetti*) used for storing betel leaves and areca nut, made of palm leaf and metal.

(Courtesy : Lilli Vijayaraghavan).

Top, left

A simple palm leaf basket

The abundance of palm trees has encouraged the use of every part of tree

Top centre

Splitting and shaving of reeds to make reed mats

Right

Woman, weaving a *korai* grass mat

Bottom

Woman weaving a screw pine mat

Screw pine is softer and more flexible but lacks the durability of *korai*.

Opposite page

Palm leaf basket-seller at an *uthsavam*

A festival is the time when business booms for indigenous basketry.

Processing of palm fibre

The palm tree is prolific in Tamilnadu and every part of it is used in some way. Its leaves are made into thin fibres and woven into bags and baskets.

Women making pith models of temples

Opposite page

Pith model of a *ther*

toys. Because it lends itself to colouring, painted pith toys are a common sight at festivals. A grain-oriented craft is that of paddy or *nellu* garlands, hung over the front door and kitchen to ward off the evil eye.

The demand for Tamilnadu's basketry and fibre products is on the increase, not only within India but also from abroad. This is hardly surprising because these crafts, depending on the ingenuity of human hands, defy competition from the mechanical sphere. Their most important aspect, however, is that they play a vital role in the rural and tribal economy, providing employment to many millions in the countryside.

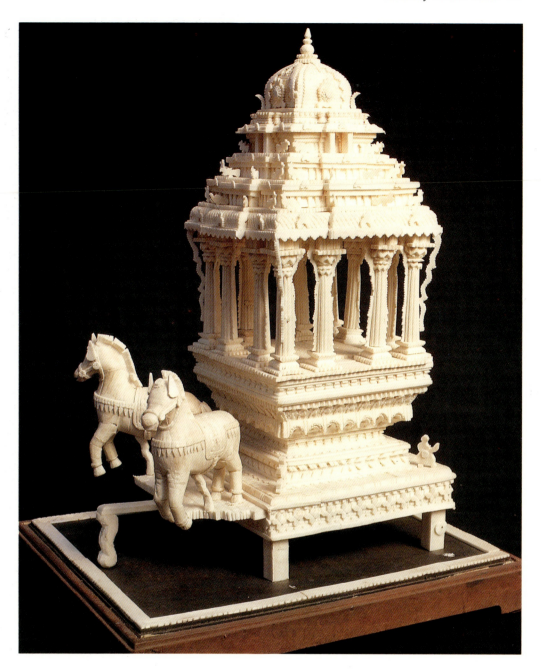

Festival Crafts & Folk Toys

In the social and economic fabric of Tamil life, festivals are occasions of the highest importance. Families are reunited, religious vows are renewed, and outlets are provided for the creative talents of the people. With special care, the housewife decorates the threshold of her home with the ritual *kolam*, tracing elaborate designs with rice flour paste. And a host of craftsmen— potters, toy-makers, sculptors — ready their wares for the seasonal markets that cater to the thousands of pilgrims who throng religious centres at festival time.

Most festivals in Tamilnadu are connected with the change of seasons or with phases of the sun and moon. Thus in January, the last day of Dakshinaayanam, or the sun's southerly course, is Bhogi-pandigai, a day that precedes Pongal, the harvest festival. The term Bhogi-pandigai literally means "the festival of physical enjoyment", and the name probably originated in the gathering in of the harvest. This festival is held in honour of Indra, god of the heavens and master of the clouds and rains, which shower abundance and prosperity over the land.

The well-known myth of Krishna and Mount Govardhana is associated with the festival. On Bhogi-pandigai day during the Dwaapara Yuga, Krishna, wanting to teach the arrogant Indra a lesson, ordered the Yadavas of Brindavan to worship the mountain instead of the god. Incensed by this, Indra caused torrential rains to flood the Yadava territory. Krishna thereupon lifted Mount Govardhana and held it aloft for the Yadavas to shelter under. Eventually Indra recognised Lord Vishnu in Krishna, repented his folly and was forgiven, and the Yadavas reverted to his worship.

According to tradition, before daybreak on the festival day, the home is thoroughly cleaned and the accumulated rubbish of the past year is burnt.

Old earthenware pots are destroyed and new ones bought. From four to six weeks earlier, the potters have been at their wheels, turning out vessels of many types. On Bhogi-pandigai, it is the custom for little boys to roam around beating the *thapatai*, a drum made of terracotta or wood with skin stretched over its ends.

The following day is Pongal, when the sun enters the zodiac house of Capricorn (*makara*). On the day of the festival, newly-harvested rice is cooked first, in fresh terracotta pots by villagers and usually in bell-metal vessels by city-dwellers. The cooked rice— also called *pongal*— is offered to the sun god as an oblation, together with newly-harvested sugarcane. The *Silappadikaaram* hails the harvest festival with the words "Praise be to the sun!"

The Pongal *pooja* is performed in the courtyard of the typical Tamilnadu house, in a spot where bright sunlight falls. The celebration of the festival varies from area to area, and each caste and community has its own special type of *kolam*. In Chettinad, *kolam* is called the *naadu-veedu* among Brahmins, and it depicts the chariot of the sun god. The doorways of houses are festooned with green mango leaves or fronds of coconut palm. And the day is considered auspicious for such ventures as sinking a well or buying a house.

The third and last day of the celebration is called Maattu Pongal (*maadu* in Tamil means a cow) after the custom of cooking *pongal* for the cows to feed on. As cattle constitute a farmer's chief asset, a day is set aside for thanksgiving to the cow. The animal is bathed, its horns are trimmed, polished, painted, and hung with brass bells, tassels, and garlands of flowers; its forehead and neck are adorned with ornaments of conch-shell. In the evening there is a staging of *jallikattu*, a uniquely

Rice flour designs

The *kolam*, design in rice flour, is drawn outside the house every morning, except during a time of mourning. Apart from signifying that all is well in the house, it is also a charm against evil spirits. There should never be loose ends, all the lines must meet, so that the evils are captured inside the *kolam* and not permitted to enter. This feat is performed by the snake, whose sinuous coils provide the basis for the patterns.

Following page

Religious procession

The procession of the Aruvathimoovar, the saints of Shaivism, who are honoured during the Panguni Uthiram Brahmothsavam in Shiva temples. The *brahmothsavam* are occasions when crafts and craftspeople can be seen in plenty (Kapaleeshwara Temple, Mylapore, Madras)

Tamil style of bull-fighting, in which the animal has to be caught bare-handed and garlanded. Formerly, a piece of cloth containing gold mohurs was tied to the horns—the reward for the young man who could overpower the bull.

Chithraa Pournami, which falls in the Chithirai (April) month of the Tamil calendar, is celebrated in honour of Chithraguptha, chief accountant of Yama, the god of death. He is said to record men's omissions and commissions in order to punish or reward them after death. To win the blessings of Chithraguptha, people draw a square *kolam* within which is a crude depiction of a man, to represent the divine accountant. A small palm and stylus—replaced today by paper and pencil—are placed in front of this *kolam*. After the *pooja*, all the family members gather before the *kolam* to invoke Chithraguptha's blessings. It is said that it was on this day, one particular year, that the constellation Chithraa, which rises over the hills at Kuttalam in Thirunelveli, made its first appearance. Hence the festival's name.

Thai Poosam is observed on the day over which the asterism Pushya(in the zodiac sign of Cancer) presides, in the Tamil month of Thai, corresponding to January-February. Legend has it that Lord Subrahmanya (Murugan) was given his *vel* (lance) by Parvati on this day, and it is celebrated with great fervour at Palani, a famous pilgrimage centre. Here, the devotees carry the icon of Murugan around the city, and the *kaavadi*, a palanquin-like structure.

The origin of the *kaavadi* is associated with the sage Agasthya who wanted to transport two hillocks to the south from Mount Kailasa. However, he was unable to proceed beyond Burchavanam and therefore sought the help of Idumban, leader of the *asuras*. To achieve his task, Idumban was invested with certain powers, with the rod of Brahma and the services of the eight serpents. The contraption he devised from these is said to resemble the modern-day *kaavadi*. Along the way, Idumban got tired and placed his burden down. This enraged Murugan, an altercation ensued, after which Idumban lost consciousness. He was restored to life only after his wife pleaded with the Lord. All this is believed to have taken place at Palani, which accounts for the festival's observance there.

Pot of sacred food

The pot contains the rice and lentil mixture called *pongal,* made during the harvest festival of the same name. As the pot overflows, signifying abundance, the onlookers shout Pongal-o-Pongal. The *kolam*-decorated brass pots are placed in the open central courtyard of the house under the sun, as Pongal is the day the sun comes to the northern hemisphere.

(Courtesy : Seetha Subbiah)

Opposite page

Wooden chariot

The *ther* or chariot, decorated with hand painted canopies and appliquéd *thombais* (cylindrical hangings), profusely carved and painted wood, and magnificent wooden springing horses, crowned by an umbrella. It is pulled along by the faithful, the very act of pulling conferring great merit.

The latent talents of the housewife are put to the test in Varalakshmi Vratham, another festival that traces its origin to legend. The story goes that Shiva and Parvati were once engaged in a game of chess. Though Parvati was winning game after game, Shiva kept claiming victory; so Parvati naturally asked for an umpire. Chithrameni was chosen for this role but, being Shiva's attendant, he unfairly supported the latter. At this, Parvati was so angry that she cursed Chithrameni and transformed him into a leper. He was forgiven only after she had extracted a promise that he would perform Varalakshmi Vratham.

This worship of the goddess of wealth is performed largely by women to invoke the blessings of Lakshmi on them, their husbands and their children, to preserve them, their *maangalya* or married status. Housewives vie with each other in drawing the *kolam* for this *pooja*, which depicts the lotus in its myriad forms. The lotus symbolises Lakshmi, patroness of farmers, who also presides over fertility and represents the umbilical cord — the life-force that sustains creation.

On the day before the *pooja*, Lakshmi's face is drawn on a *kumbha* (a terracotta pot), into which lime, rice and a few coins have been dropped and which is topped with mango leaves and a coconut smeared with turmeric and sandalwood paste. Then, on a silver pot covered with sandal paste, the face of Lakshmi is painted — the eyes with *maiyi* or collyrium, the lips with red *kumkum*, the nose and ears with turmeric. She is adorned with jewellery and flowers. Sometimes a bejewelled silver mask is used instead and the pot is covered with a skirt. The mask, the terracotta pot and silver vessel all provide occupation for the craftsman.

Gokulaashtami celebrates the birth of Lord Krishna which falls on the *ashtami* or the eighth day of the month Aavani (August-September). The *kolam* leading to the prayer room traces the outline of small feet, signifying the entry of the infant Krishna into the house. Special food particular to this *pooja*, such as *cheedai, murukku* and milk sweets, are offered as oblations.

Vinayaka Pillaiyaar, Ganapathi or Ganesha is the most popular deity of Tamilnadu, and even the smallest hamlet has a temple for his worship.

Also celebrated in the month of Aavani; his *pooja* is performed to acquire strength of will for success in all undertakings. The well-known story of how Ganesha has an elephant head may be recalled briefly. Asked by Parvati to guard her bathing quarters, Ganesha refused Shiva admission, for which he was beheaded. It was only in response to Parvati's entreaties that Shiva asked his attendants to go to the forest and bring back the head of the first living being they saw, which happened to be an elephant. And this is how the elephant head was placed on Ganapathi's shoulders.

In the villages, Vinayaka Chathurthi offers ample scope for the people's creativity. All the children try to fashion the clay. Ganesha—his elephant face, his trunk curved at the tip, the crown, his four arms, one holding a *modaka,* his favourite sweet, big belly, two stumpy legs, and his *vaahana,* the *mooshika* (mouse or shrew).

The scarlet and black-eyed seeds of the *kunrimani* (crab's eye) are used as Vinayaka's eyes. Formerly, the figures were made out of the mud of an ant-hill, but nowadays clay has taken over. The *kudai* (umbrella), a contemporary addition, is made of crepe paper and coloured tassels. Unable to cope with the demand for the idol, the craftsmen now use moulds on which they hand-press the pliable clay to cast the image.

Perhaps the festival dearest to Tamil hearts is Navaraathri (nine nights) or Bommai Kolu — the festival of dolls — observed for nine days starting soon after the new moon of the Tamil month Purattaasi (September-October). In each household, a wide stepped stand is erected to display the dolls. These represent the various gods and goddesses which are arranged to depict stories from the epics and the *Puraanas. Kolu* is planned in an almost competitive spirit — the bigger the dolls, the greater is the householder's social standing— and the occasion provides an opportunity for doll-makers to excel. Even in temples, a grand display of *kolu* is set out.

Traditionally, the dolls are made of terracotta and then painted. Each craftsman produces a few new moulds every season to add to his already existing stock. The *kolu* presents a great variety — oscillating toys from Thanjavur, clay toys from Panruti, papier-maché toys, miniature household articles, animals and birds and many more.

The festival is in honour of the Mother Goddess in her varied aspects — Durga, Lakshmi and Saraswati. The nine days are equally distributed between these three, and the tenth is considered a day of victory, when evil was overpowered by the Supreme Mother. On *navami,* the ninth day, people worship the tools of their trade.

On the tenth day, or Vijaya-dashami, Rama's *pattaabhishekam* (coronation) is celebrated in most Tamil houses. It is believed that Rama himself celebrated Vasantha Navaraathri in the forest while looking for Seetha, and that he returned to Ayodhya victorious on the tenth day along with her. On this auspicious day, new business ventures, the *aksharaabhyaasa* (the first learning of the alphabet), or the first music lesson are begun.

Deepavali, the festival of lights, is also called Naraka Chathurdasi in Tamilnadu. According to legend, Naraka, a demon ruling over parts of East India, started wreaking havoc upon men and gods. They sought Krishna's intercession, and it was on the third day before dawn that the demon was destroyed. Naraka's last prayer was that those who observed this day with a ritual bath, feasting and fireworks would go to heaven.

Celebrations begin a fortnight before Deepavali with special bazaars set up to sell fireworks. These herald the victory of Krishna over Naraka, and they must be lit before the coming of dawn. As it is the monsoon period in Tamilnadu, the fireworks substitute for the *deepam* (lamp), rows of which light up the festival in the north. Months before the festival, the crackers start being hand-made at Sivakasi, the country's largest fireworks producer.

Also called the festival of lights in Tamilnadu is Kaarthigai Deepam, which falls in the month of Kaarthigai (November-December). An outstanding feature of this celebration is the huge lamp that is lit high on a hill at Thiruvannamalai, a place sanctified by its enormous temple to Shiva. In the home, women light row upon row of terracotta lamps (*man-vilakku)* as well as large brass lamps called *kuthu-vilakku.* Potters and metal-

Shiva's vehicle

Adhikaara Nandi, the bull of Shiva, who is one of the *vaahanas* or vehicles of Shiva during the Panguni Uthiram festival. The figure is made of wood and covered with silver, giving Nandi an imperious look. Other crafts, such as floral decorations and *kolam*, are given an impetus at this time.

workers are hard at work during this season producing all manner of lamps for the festival, because a new lamp, whether of terracotta or metal, has to be bought and lit along with the older ones.

The same craftsmen are also kept busy making the *karagam*, an observance associated with the cult of Mariamman. The *karagam* consists of terracotta or brass vessels, tapering in size and placed one on top of the other. It is crowned with a small tower of neem leaves smeared with saffron and vermilion. The *karagam* is carried on the head of a devotee, who is usually dressed like a warrior and who sometimes performs acrobatics while balancing the vessels. Known as *aatta-karagam,* this balancing act is accompanied by special musical instruments — the *pampaadi, urumi, thavil, naadaswaram,* and *thamakku.*
In addition to individual celebrations, there are periods of community worship and festivities in Tamilnadu. Called *brahmothsavams,* these are observed at different times in different parts of the state and last for 10 to 15 days.

The *brahmothsavam* at Madurai falls in the Vaikaasi month of the Tamil calendar (May-June) and the Panguni Uthiram, honouring Parvati's devotion to Shiva, is held during Panguni (March-April). The main feature of this celebration is that the presiding deity, his consorts, and lesser deities are taken around the streets in the *ther* or *ratham.* Every day for a fortnight, the deities are elaborately decorated with flowers and jewels and paraded in his or her particular *vaahana* or vehicle. On the last day, only the temple's presiding deity and his or her consort are carried ceremonially in procession. A unique aspect of the Panguni Uthiram is that the *vaaha-nas,* which are nearly three metres in height, commemorate the well-known devotees of Shiva, from Nandi to Ravana. On one day, the 63 Naayanmaars or saints of Shaivism are honoured as 63 individual icons. On the last day, the *ther* is dragged through the streets by the devotees.

A product of skilled craftsmanship, the *ther* is built of wood with intricate designs and carvings. An ornamental canopy rises tier upon tier to assume towering dimensions. Colourful appliqued *thoranams* (lintel pieces) and *thombais* (long, cylindrical hangings) are suspended from the *ther,*

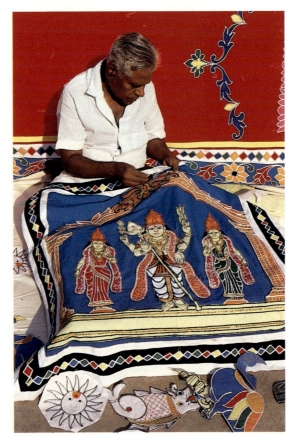

Top

Puppetry-making, Pondicherry.

The puppets are marionettes with papier-mache heads and cloth bodies. The ones made at Pondicherry are a coming-together of Indian traditions and French influences

(Courtesy : Project Yosanai)

Applique craftsman C. Swaminathan at work on a wall panel

Opposite page

The coronation of Rama

Painted wooden figures decorated with cut glass depict the coronation of Rama. Exclusive to Thanjavur, cut-glass work involves the embellishment of wooden articles with colourful pieces of broken or cut glass and gold or silver paper or foil.

which is dragged along by people by means of thick palm-fibre ropes. This is the time not only for worship and prayer but also for the craftsmen to sell their wares to the devotees who have gathered for the temple car festival.

The various Muslim festivals also provide an opportunity to witness the high quality of festival crafts. Thus, during the annual Kandoori celebrations in memory of Saint Quadar Wali, green flags decorated with wooden ships are carried in procession from Nagapattinam to Nagore. This perpetuates the legend attributed to the saint who saved a ship from sinking near Singapore after he had seen a vision.

An annual Christian festival held at Velanganni near Nagapattinam honours Mary, known as Annai Velanganni by the local population. Mary is said to have great healing powers and many pilgrims go to the church, light candles, and take a vow to offer the limb or afflicted part in gold or silver, if cured of the ailment. There is therefore a large market for gold and silver workers who fashion these delicate pieces. Candle-making is also one of the chief occupations of the people of Velanganni.

Festival days in Tamilnadu reveal the great wealth of the state's arts and crafts. More important, they draw attention to the importance of the craftsman in the religious and social life of the people. For it is he who creates the image which the priest will later imbue with divinity.

*

Tamilnadu provides a rich panorama of toys fashioned out of almost every conceivable material, from clay to cloth. Each of these represents a splendid synthesis of folk art and nature, the essence of which permeates the toy, making it at once vital and vibrant.

The most popular of these toys are made of clay and terracotta, an industry that has been firmly established in Pondicherry, Madras, Kanchipuram, and parts of Arcot. The craft pockets situated in these areas are of ancient origin, the craft itself being a hereditary tradition in the artisan's family.

The toy industry in Pondicherry is several centuries old and, though predominantly based on

The many uses of shells

Shell toys, consisting of either large individual shells or small ones stuck together to form an animal or person, are cheap and easy to make.

Opposite page , top

Children's entertainment

This is a unique home-made parrot, very popular among women and children who make such figures to entertain themselves. The green body is made up of leaves, pomegranate skin forms the eyes, neck band and beak, and painted twigs the feet.

Opposite page, Centre

Dynamic indigenous toys made of paper, twigs and wire

These are facing extinction today and appear only at *uthsavams*.

Real life miniaturised in toys

This *vaahana* or vehicle, made of painted wood, can be pulled along on wheels by the enterprising child who wants to re-create his own *uthsavam* or festival at home.

clay, has today expanded to include papier-maché and plaster of Paris toys. It is largely concentrated in Kosapalayam, the craftsmen belonging to the Kosavan or Kuyavan community. The range extends from religious toys to household items and animals, painted in natural earthy tints. Today, a large variety of toys are coloured with enamel paints.

There is, however, an established convention under which certain colours are used to depict men and women in different walks of life. A rich orange indicates men and women of the priestly class, while greys and russet indicate those engaged in manual labour. In the case of a groom and bride, they and the entire bridal entourage are resplendent in shimmering orange or pink. The affluent characters are differentiated by the colour and brightness of their clothing from the lesser folk who are painted in grey, to highlight the difference. Thus, at no juncture does the craftsman lose touch with reality and, even as the child is transported from this world to the sphere of imagination, he passes through a process of learning with these toys.

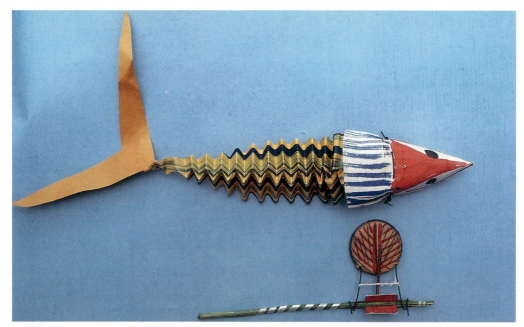

The sales are seasonal, but with the onset of Navaraathri and the *kolu* (doll) festival the trade thrives and sales are very brisk. Apart from the painted clay toys, Pondicherry was once known for its painted or gilt-covered wooden toys. This craft is practically extinct today.

In Madras, the clay toy industry represents an array of the celestial and the supernatural, and the toys are manufactured by about 300 artisan families from Cuddalore, now settled in Kosapet. Kanchipuram is yet another centre of clay toy-making.

Clay toys are manufactured in two distinct stages: the preparation of the mould and the colouring of the finished products. Plaster of Paris is mixed with tapioca powder and then made into a paste and dried till it can be rolled into layers. This is then pressed into the die and the necessary moulds are obtained. The raw material used for the manufacture of these toys is rock clay. The moist clay is, in turn, pressed into the mould which, prior to this, is dusted with French chalk so that the end products can be easily detached. Once removed, they are exposed to sunlight for a day. The dried clay toys are now ready for colouring.

While the men knead the clay, roll it into layers, make the moulds and models, the women transform the drab clay into richly-coloured toys with their brushes dipped in paints contained in coconut shells. The children are also actively involved in the process, performing odd jobs, cleaning, and so on. The finishing touches are given by the women, supervised by the master craftsmen.

Lathe-turned, lacquered, wooden toys, particularly miniature cooling vessels and walkers, are known as *kadasal*. These are brightly coloured, inexpensive and very popular all over the state. Soapstone (*maakal*) is also used for making miniature cooking utensils.

Panruti, near Cuddalore in South Arcot district, is famous for its clay toys, many of which are still painted with vegetable colours. And Karigiri, near Vellore, is known particularly for its toy animals. Madurai has a unique centre which specialises in a large variety of metal creations, particularly brass insects, remarkably lifelike because of careful attention to detail.

Thanjavur was once reputed for its elegant and excellent oscillating toys, now concentrated more in the neighbouring districts of Kumbakonam and Mayavaram. The famous dancing doll of Thanjavur, though not exactly a toy, nevertheless deserves mention. This is made of papier-maché : the paper pulp is mixed with clay and applied to a cut mould by hand, a process involving great skill and delicacy of touch. The doll is made in four parts: the circular base with the legs attached, the lower part of the body from the waist downward, the upper body and arms, and the head. Each part is delicately balanced on wires so that the slightest touch sets the whole doll dancing.

The making of pith toys centres chiefly around Kumbakonam. Pith is the hard core of a water reed found profusely in tanks, swamps and lakes in Thanjavur district. The reed is gathered and dried till all the superfluous hair is shed. The ivory coloured reed, which is soft, smooth and extremely pliable, is then fashioned into various playthings.

Mannapadu is known for toy animals made out of palm leaf. The leaves, dipped in appropriate colour dyes, are interwoven so as to transform the original leaf into splendid and fanciful creations. Sometimes, the stem of the leaf is used for further strength and support.

Almost all these are cottage industries, and the craft is pursued by the family of the craftsman at his residence. Very few are employed from outside, the art by and large being the sole prerogative of the craftmen's kith and kin. In a way, in the remotest parts of Tamilnadu, the practice of toy-making jointly, as in the case of other crafts, has helped bring the family much closer, re-establishing family ties and accentuating it as one group, an exlcusive unit.

A silver *kodam* or pot decorated as Varalakshmi, worshipped by married women as a protector of their *maangalyam* (married status). The decoration is done using turmeric, collyrium and vermilion powder (kumkum).
Courtesy : Nanditha Krishna

Glossary of Proper Names

Aanamalai: the elephant hills, a mountain range which extends towards Travancore

Aavadaiyar: a name of Shiva, the presiding deity of a temple in Karaikudi

Adhikaara Nandi: a form of Nandi, the Bull, the *vaahana* of Shiva during the Panguni Uthiram Festival in Shiva Temples (March-April), when Nandi is given greater importance than his Lord

Adichanallur: an important archaeological site on the banks of the river Thaamraparni

Adithya: a Chola king who ruled between AD 871 and 907

Agasthya: a *rishi* venerated in Tamil literature as the first codifier of Tamil grammar, a lost treatise known as the Agathiyam. He is believed to have led the first migration of Tamils to South India

Agathiyam: Tamil grammatical treatise, now lost, believed to have been written by sage Agasthya

Agni: the God of Fire, one of the chief deities of the Vedas

Aihole: an important architectural centre of the early Western Chalukyas, now in Northern Karnataka

Airavatheshvara: another name of Lord Shiva

Akshisuthra: a canon of iconography

Alagarai: an archaeological site in Tamilnadu

Amrithamangalam: a town in Chingleput district of Tamilnadu

Anantha: the name of the serpent who forms the couch of Lord Vishnu

Annai Velanganni: Virgin Mary as she is known in a famous church at Velanganni near Nagapattinam

Arcot: a town in North Arcot district

Ardhanarishvara: a form in which Shiva is represented as half-male and half-female, typifying the male and female energies

Arikamedu: an archaeological site near Pondicherry, with artefacts of Roman trade

Ariyalur: a town in Thiruchirapalli district

Arjuna: the third Pandava Prince from the epic *Mahabharatha*

Arni : a place in North Arcot district famous for silk sarees known as Arni silk

Aruvalar: a caste of cultivators from Orissa

Aruvathimoovar: the sixty-three saints of Tamil Shaivism also known as Naayanmaar

Ashoka: celebrated king who lived between 234 and 198 BC

Auroville: an international township in Pondicherry

Ayodhya: the modern Oudh and afterwards the capital of Rama

Ayyampettai: a village in Thanjavur district

Badagas: a tribe in the Nilgiris district

Badami: the capital of the early Western Chalukyas, now in Northern Karnataka

Balakrishna: Lord Krishna as a child

Bhairavar: a form of Shiva

Bharatha Natyam: the classical dance form of Tamilnadu

Bhavani: a town near Salem famous for its durries

Bhumisuthra: a canon of iconography

Bommi: a village spirit, wife of Madurai Veeran

Brahma: the Creator, according to Hindu tradition

Brahmapuram: a village near Nagerkoil

Brahmi: the earliest Indian script from which all Indian scripts are derived

Brahmin: the first of four main castes of Hindu society; the early Brahmins were priests and teachers

Brahul: a language of Dravidian origin now found in Baluchistan (Pakistan)

Brihadeeshvara: Shiva as he is known in the Great Temple of Thanjavur

Brihath Samhitha: a famous treatise on astronomy by Varahamihira, who lived in the fifth century AD

Brindavan: a village on the banks of the river Yamuna believed to be the home of Lord Krishna

Budha: the planet Mercury

Burchavanam: a village near Palani, beyond which sage Agasthya was unable to take the two hillocks which he brought from Mount Kailasa to the south

Chalukyas: an ancient dynasty which ruled Northern Karnataka from the 6th to 8th centuries

Chandesaanugrahamurthi: a name of Shiva, as he grants a boon to his devotee Chandesa

Chandra: the moon

Cheethalaichaathanar: the author of *Manimekhalai* a Tamil epic

Cheras: an ancient ruling dynasty of Tamilnadu

Chettiar: a trading community of Tamilnadu

Chettinad: a part of Pasumpon Muthuramalingam district inhabited predominantly by the Nagarathaars.

Chidambaram: a town in South Arcot district in which the famous temple of Lord Nataraja is situated

Chingleput: a district in Tamilnadu

Chithraguptha: Chief Accountant of Yama, the God of Death, who is said to record men's omissions and commissions

Chithrameni: Shiva's attendant

Chittan: a village spirit

Chola: An ancient ruling dynasty of Tamilnadu

Cholamandalam: the kingdom of the Cholas which approximately corresponds to the rice-growing belt between Thiruchirapalli and the Kaveri Delta

Coimbatore: a major industrial center of Tamilnadu

Coromandel Coast: the coast of Tamilnadu where it meets the Bay of Bengal

C.P. Ramaswami Aiyar: the former Dewan of Travancore in whose name there is a Foundation in Madras city

Cuddalore: a town in South Arcot district of Tamilnadu

Daksha: the father of Uma, a form of Shiva's wife Parvati

Darasuram: a village in Thanjavur district

Daksha: the father of Uma, a form of Shiva's wife Parvati

Darasuram: a village in Thanjavur district

Daripatnam: a village in Ramnad district

Devakottai: a part of Ramanathapuram district

Devangar: a weaving community

Devi: the Mother Goddess

Dharmapuri: a district of Tamilnadu

Draupadi: the wife of the five Pandavas of the epic *Mahabharatha*

Dravidian: a linguistic group to which the Tamil language belongs

Durga: the great Goddess, wife of Shiva. She rides a lion and carries a trident in her hand

Ekambareshwara: another name for Shiva, Lord of a temple of the same name at Kanchipuram

Elamites: a people of ancient Mesopotamia

Erode: a district of Tamilnadu named after the town Erode

Ettuthohai: eight anthologies or a collection of selected poems

Eyinar: a Naga tribe of Tamilnadu

Gajalakshmi: a form of Goddess Lakshmi flanked by two elephants

Gajasamhaaramurti : Shiva as the destroyer of the elephant demon

Ganapathi: see Ganesha

Ganesha: a god, son of Lord Shiva and Parvati

Ganga: a sacred river in Northern and Eastern India

Gangaikondachola: a title of Rajendra I, a Chola king who ruled from AD 1012 to 1044

Gangaikondacholapuram: a village in Thanjavur district, once the capital of Rajendra Chola I

Garuda: the eagle kite, vehicle of Lord Vishnu

Garudaalwaar: Garuda as an Aalwaar or devotee of Lord Vishnu

Gayathri: the most sacred verse of the Vedas, invoking the Sun

Gingee: a town in South Arcot district

Govardhana: a hill which was lifted and held as an umbrella by Lord Krishna

Guru: the planet Jupiter

Harappa: the site of the ancient Indus Valley culture of India

Hassan Bawa Labbai: a Muslim mat weaver of Pathamadai who lived in the nineteenth century and is credited with the creation of the silky, soft Pathamadai mats

Heramba: five-headed Ganesha, seated on the lion

Hurrians: an ancient people who once lived along the Euphrates river

Idumban: leader of the *asuras*

Ilango Adigal: author of *Silappadikaaram*

Indra: the god of the firmament who reigns over the heavens. He was once the chief god of the Vedas

Isakai Amman: a village goddess

Jacquard: fabric with figured weave

Jambai: a village in South Arcot district

Jambudvipa: one of the seven islands or continents of which the world is made up

Kadars: a tribal community of Aanamalais

Kaikolar: a weaver community

Kailasa: the abode of Shiva

Kakshasuthra: a canon of iconography

Kalabhras: an unpopular tribe which ruled Tamilnadu between AD 300 and 600

Kaali: the Mother Goddess

Kalinga: the contemporary state of Orissa

Kaveripattinam: also called Kaveripoompattinam, the ancient city of Poompuhar submerged in the sea

Kaveripoompattinam: see Kaveripattinam

Ketu: a snake divinity, one of the nine planets

Kharavela: a king of Kalinga (Orissa) who reigned in the second century BC

Kaliyamardhana Krishna: Lord Krishna dancing on the serpent Kaliya

Kalugumalai: an archaeological site in Thirunelveli district

Kamaladevi Chattopadhyay: the first Chairman of the all-India Handicrafts Board

Kammalar: caste of sculptors

Kampahareshvara: another name of Shiva

Kanchi: see Kanchipuram

Kanchipuram: a town in Chingleput district of Tamilnadu

Kannagi: the heroine of *Silappadikaaram,* a Tamil epic

Kanniamman: a village goddess

Kanyakumari: a district of Tamilnadu, a town at the tip of the subcontinent

Kapaleeshwara Temple: the great Shiva Temple in Mylapore, Madras

Karaikudi: a town in Chettinad

Karigiri: a village in North Arcot district

Karthikeya: the God of War, also a form of Lord Subrahmanya, and the son of Lord Shiva

Karukas : community of weavers

Karumaariamman: a village goddess

Karupoor: a village in Thanjavur district

Karuppan: a village deity

Karur: a town in Thiruchirapalli district

Kassites: an ancient tribe of Southern Iran

Kauravas: descendants of Kuru, generally applied to the sons of Dhritharashtra, of the epic *Mahabharatha*

Kautilya: author of the *Artha Shastra,* a classic treatise on political economy; he lived in the third century BC

Kaveri: a river in South India

Killi-Valavan: an ancient Chola King

Kodali-Karupoor: name of saree from Karupoor village, Thanjavur district

Kodambakkam: a part of Madras city

Kodiakkadu: a village in Thanjavur district

Komatis: a sub-caste of Chettiars

Konarak: the site of the Sun Temple in Orissa

Kondapalli: a place in Andhra Pradesh, famous for its wooden toys

Kongu-Cheramandalam: the area around Coimbatore and Dharmapuri districts of Tamilnadu, once ruled by the Cheras

Kosapalayam: an area in Pondicherry

Kosapet: see Kosapalayam

Kosavan: potter

Kotas: a tribe of the Nilgiris

Kottaiyur: a village near Kumbakonam

Kovalan : hero of *Silappadikaaram*

Krishna: an incarnation of Lord Vishnu and one of the chief gods of contemporary Hinduism

Krishnapuram: an architectural site in Thirunelveli district

Kshatriyas: the warrior caste

Kuayiamman: a village goddess

Kuja: the planet Mars

Kulalaar : potter

Kumbakonam: a town in Thanjavur district

Kunrathur: a village in Chingleput district

Kurainadu: a village in Mayavaram taluk of Thanjavur district

Kurthunaikkanpatti: a village in Salem district

Kuttalam: a town in Thirunelveli district

Kuyavan : potter

Lakshmi: goddess of prosperity, wife of Lord Vishnu

Lambadis: a nomadic tribe

Limurike: an ancient name for Tamilnadu used by the Greeks

Lingodhbhava: a form of Shiva as he emerges from the *linga*

Maanasara: a canon of architecture

Maarar: an ancient tribe of Tamilnadu

Madhavi: the dancing girl in the epic *Silappadikaaram*

Madurai Veeran: a popular ancient village spirit and folk hero, now deified

Madurai: a town and district of Tamilnadu

Mahabalipuram: see Mamallapuram

Mahabharatha: an important Sanskrit epic

Mahisha: the buffalo demon who is killed by goddess Durga

Mahishasuramardhini: Durga as the killer of the buffalo demon

Mamallapuram: an architectural site, also known as Mahabalipuram, in Chingleput district, Tamilnadu

Mannapadu: a village in Thanjavur district

Maravar: a tribe living around Madurai

Maariamman: a village goddess

Mathura: the ancient name for the contemporary town of Madurai of Tamilnadu

Manamadurai: a village in Ramnad district

Manija: probably a landlord

Manimekhalai: an epic on the daughter of Kovalan and Madhavi of the epic *Silappadikaaram*

Mathurapathi: a woman ruler of Madurai, founder of the Pandya dynasty

Maulisuthra: a canon of iconography

Mayamatha: a Tamil canon of sculpture belonging to the tenth century AD

Mayavaram: a taluk in Thanjavur district

Meenakshi Amman Temple: the temple of goddess Meenakshi at Madurai

Meenakshi: the goddess of the huge temple at Madurai

Meenavar: fishermen

Melakkadambur: the site of a Chola temple, near Chidambaram in South Arcot district

Mookambika: a village goddess

Moothan Kaali: a village goddess

Moplah: Kerala Muslim

Muhandanur: a village in Thanjavur district

Mummadi Krishnaraja Wodeyar: an eighteenth century ruler of Mysore State, famous for his patronage of religion, literature and the arts

Muniyaandi: a spirit, generally an attendant of Madurai Veeran

Muniyappa: a village spirit

Murugan: another name for Lord Subrahmanya, son of Lord Shiva

Muthunaikanpatti: a village in Salem district

Mylapore: a part of Madras city

Naabhisuthra: a canon of iconography

Naattukottai Chettiar: the Nagarathaar sub-division of the Chettiars

Naayan: another name for Lord Shiva

Naayanmaar: Shaivite saints

Nachiarkoil: a village in Thanjavur district, where bell metal casting is done

Naga: an ancient tribe, frequently mentioned in Tamil and Sanskrit literature

Nagapattinam: a town in Thanjavur district

Nagarathaar Chettiars: a sub-sect of Chettiars

Nagarathaars: a trading community of Tamilnadu, also known as Chettiars

Nagerkoil: a town and headquarters of Kanyakumari district

Nagore: a town in Thanjavur district

Namakkal: a village near Salem with ninth and tenth century cave sculptures

Nandi: the chief attendant and vehicle of Lord Shiva

Naraka: a demon, believed to rule the underworld, whose destruction by Krishna is the cause for celebration during Deepavali

Narasimha: the man-lion incarnation of Lord Vishnu

Nari Kuravas: fox-gypsies of Tamilnadu, so-called because of their fox hunting

Nataraja: Lord Shiva as the divine dancer

Naatya Shaastra: Canon on dance

Nayaks: local chieftains of Tamilnadu during the reign of the Vijayanagara Kingdom, who became the rulers of city-states after the collapse of Vijayanagara in the sixteenth century

Nilgiris: hill range in Tamilnadu forming a part of the Western Ghats

Oliyar: a tribe of Tamilnadu

Omalur: a town in Salem district

Oviyanul: a Tamil treatise on painting

Oviyar: a tribe of Tamilnadu

Paalayankkottai: a fort in Thirunelveli district

Padinenkizhkanakku: a Tamil anthology of eighteen poems

Padmanabhapuram: the palace of the erstwhile kings of Travancore

Padma-Sale: a community of weavers

Padmasura: a demon who was destroyed by Lord Shiva

Paiyampalli: an ancient Megalithic site dating back to the Neolithic period

Palani: a famous pilgrimage centre near Madurai

Paleacate: a town on the Coromandel Coast better known as Pulicat

Pallathur: a village in Chettinad

Pallava: an ancient ruling dynasty of Tamilnadu

Pancha Pandava Ratha: the monolithic temples built by the Pallavas in the seventh century AD at Mamallapuram

Pandaia: a daughter of Herakles (or Krishna), referred to by Megasthenes, the Greek ambassador who visited the court of Chandragupta Maurya

Pandavas: the descendants (sons) of Pandu, King of Hasthinapura

Pandiamandalam: the kingdom of the Pandvas corresponding roughly to the area around Madurai

Pandoe: a race ruled by women, probably the Pandyas

Pandyas: an ancient ruling dynasty of Tamilnadu

Panruti: a village in South Arcot district

Papanasam: a village in Thanjavur district

Parashurama: the sixth incarnation of Lord Vishnu

Parathavar: a Tamil tribe

Paranthaka: a Chola king who ruled between AD 907 and 955

Parvati: the consort of Lord Shiva

Pathamadai: a village in Thirunelveli district famous for its mats.

Pathupaattu: a Tamil anthology of ten poems

Pattadakkal: a site of Western Chalukyan architecture now in Northern Karnataka

Pattabhi Rama: Rama, crowned king

Pattu-Sale: a community of silk weavers

Pattunulkaras: a weaving community

Pidaari: a village goddess

Pillaiyaar: another name for Lord Ganesha

Pillaiyarpatti: a village in Thiruchirapalli district

Pondicherry: a Union Territory adjoining South Arcot district once occupied by the French

Ponneri: a village in South Arcot district of Tamilnadu

Poompuhar: an ancient Tamil city, also known as Kaveripattinam or Kaveripoompattinam, at the mouth of the Kaveri, once the capital of the Pandyas; it was destroyed by the sea

Pooranai: a village Goddess, one of the consorts of Ayyanaar

Porunarrupadai: one of the *Pathupaattu*

Prakrit: provincial dialect of Sanskrit

Puduchheri: another name for Pondicherry

Pudukottai: a town in Pudukottai district of Tamilnadu

Puhar: the ancient town of Poompuhar or Kaveripoompattinam destroyed by the sea

Pulicat: a town on the Coromandel Coast

Quadar Wali: a Muslim saint whose tomb is in Nagore

Raghunatha Nayak: a Nayak ruler of Thanjavur who ruled in the 17th century

Rahu: a snake divinity, one of the nine planets

Rajakesarivarman Perumanadigal king : another name for Rajaraja Chola

Rajaraja Chola: a Chola king who ruled from AD 985 to 1016

Rajendra: a Chola king son of Rajaraja who ruled from AD 1012 to 1044

Rajarajeshwari: one of the names of Devi or the Mother goddess

Raju: a Telugu-speaking community of painters who are believed to have come from the kingdom of Vijayanagara

Rama: an incarnation of Vishnu, the hero of Ramayana

Ramanathapuram: the headquarters of Ramanathapuram (Ramnad) district

Ramaswamy: Lord of the Ramaswamy temple at Kumbakonam, Thanjavur district

Ramayana: an important Sanskrit epic

Rameshwaram: a pilgrimage centre on the South Eastern coast of Tamilnadu where Rama is stated to have consecrated and worshipped the *lingam*

Ramnad: a district of Tamilnadu

Ranganatha: the form of Lord Vishnu as he reclines on the serpent Anantha. The Lord of the temple at Srirangam near Thiruchirappalli

Ravana: king of Lanka who was defeated by Rama

Ravi: the sun

Renuka Devi: a village goddess, Mother of Parashurama

Saidapet: a part of Madras city

Salava: a community of weavers

Salem: a district of Tamilnadu

Saliyar: a community of weavers

Sangam: an ancient conference of Tamil language and literature

Sani: the planet Saturn

Sanskrit: the ancient language of the Indo-Aryans

Sanur: a megalithic site in Chingleput district

Saraswathi: the goddess of learning according to Hindu tradition

Satiyaputa: a kingdom outside the Ashokan Empire comprising roughly the Salem and Coimbatore districts

Saurashtra: a community of weavers originally from Saurashtra in Gujarat.

Seetha: the heroine of *Ramayana;* Rama's wife

Sembiyan Mahadevi: wife of Gandaraditya, son of Paranthaka Chola she was a great patron of religion who built several temples between AD 955 and 985

Sengundam Mudaliar: a community of weavers

Seniyar: a community of weavers

Serfoji Maharaja: the Maratha king who ruled over Thanjavur in the 18th century

Shaivite: follower of Shiva

Shakthi: the Mother Goddess, symbolic of power

Shakthi Ganesha: a form of Ganesha with Shakthi the Mother Goddess sitting on his knee

Shakthimuni: a village spirit

Shankarankovil: a town in Thirunelveli district

Shanmugha: another name for Karthikeya, son of Lord Shiva

Shilpa Shaastra : canon of sculpture

Shilparathna: a canon of iconography

Shiva: the Destroyer, according to Hindu tradition

Shudra: one of the castes of Hindu society

Shukra: the planet Venus

Sickinaikenpet: a village near Thanjavur which is the only location of kalamkari in Tamilnadu

Silappadikaaram: a Tamil classic presenting the popular epic of Kovalan and Kannagi

Sirgazhi Temple: the site of a Chola temple in Thanjavur district

Sittannavasal: the site of Jain paintings of the Pandyan period

Sivakasi: a town in Ramnad district which is the country's largest producer of fireworks

Skanda: another name for Karthikeya, son of Lord Shiva

Skandapurana: a collection of legends named after Skanda

Srikaraimal Azhakar: a temple in Thanjavur

Srirangam: a place near Thiruchirapalli which is the site of the Sri Ranganatha temple

Subrahmanya: another name for Karthikeya, son of Lord Shiva

Surya: the sun

Sushrutha Samhitha: a treatise on Ayurveda, ancient Indian form of herbal medicine

Swamimalai: a village outside Kumbakonam in Thanjavur district, which is an important site of bronze casting in Tamilnadu.

Talikota: the site of a terrible battle in 156⟨ which resulted in the rout of the Vijayanagara army and the destruction of the Vijayanagara kingdom

Tamilaham: the home of the Tamils or Tamilnadu

Tanjore: another name for Thanjavur

Thaamraparni: a river in Thirunelveli district

Thanjavur: a town and district in Tamilnadu

Thathaiyampatti: a village near Omalur

Thevaram: an ancient Tamil Shaivite work

Thirayar: an ancient tribe of Tamilnadu from whom the Pallavas and Cholas claimed descent

Thiruchirapalli: an important town and headquarters of Thiruchirapalli district in Tamilnadu

Thirugnanasambandhar: one of the sixty-three Naayanmaars

Thirukkampuliyur: an early archaeological site in Tamilnadu

Thirukkural: a Tamil code of ethics

Thirumala Nayak: the ruler of Madurai in the 17th century

Thirunelveli: a town of Tamilnadu, the headquarters of Thirunelveli district

Thiruvakkarai: a site of a Shiva temple in Thanjavur district

Thiruvannamalai: a pilgrimage town in North Arcot district of Tamilnadu

Thiruvarur: the site of a Shiva temple in Thanjavur district

Thiruvengadu: the site of a Shiva temple in Thanjavur district

Thiruverkadu: a village in Chingleput district

Tholkaapiyam: a treatise of grammar of the third or fourth century AD

Thondaimandalam: the northern part of the Tamil country

Thribhuvanam: a site of a Shiva temple in Thanjavur district

Tippu Sultan: ruler of Mysore from 1783 to 1799

Todas: a tribe in the Nilgiris district

Travancore: a state in south western India now forming part of Kerala state and Tamilnadu

Trichinopoly: the anglicised name for Thiruchirapalli

Tuticorin: an important port in Thirunelveli district

Uma Maheshwara: the form of Shiva and Parvati seated on Nandi

Uraiyur: an ancient centre of cotton weaving in Thiruchirapalli district

Uruvaram: a terracotta figure of a female guardian of children

Vaanavar: an ancient tribe of Tamilnadu

Vaishnavite: followers of Lord Vishnu

Vaishyas: a trading caste of Tamilnadu

Valampuri Ganesha: a form of Ganesha with the trunk curved to the right

Vallamuni: a village spirit

Vamuni: a village spirit

Varadaraaja: a form of Vishnu

Varadaraajaswami Temple: the temple of Vishnu as Lord Varadaraaja in Kanchipuram

Varahamihira: an astronomer who lived in the 6th century AD

Varahalakshmi : Lakshmi

Varkalpet: a village near Cuddalore in South Arcot district

Vedas: the sacred revelations of the Hindus

Veerabhadra: he is believed to have sprung from the third eye of Lord Shiva to kill Daksha, Shiva's father-in-law

Velanganni: the site of the famous church of Velanganni near Nagappattinam in Thanjavur district

Velar : potter

Vellalas: an agricultural community of Tamilnadu

Vellore: the headquarters of North Arcot district of Tamilnadu

Venugopala: the form of Krishna playing the flute

Vettuvankovil: the site of rock sculptures near Kalugumalai

Vibheeshana: the brother of Ravana, villain of the *Ramayana*

Vigneshwara: another name for Lord Ganesha

Vijayanagara: a powerful kingdom which led the Hindu revival between AD 1336 and 1564.

Villavar: an ancient (bow-men) tribe of Tamilnadu

Villukkatti Ayyanaar Koil : a temple at Varkalpet near Cuddalore in South Arcot district

Vinayaka: another name for Ganesha

Vindhyas: a hill range in Central India

Vishnu: the god of preservation according to Hindu tradition

Vishwakarma : the architect of the gods, identified as the creator

Vivekananda: a famous monk of the Ramakrishna Mission

Yadavas: a tribe to which Lord Krishna belonged

Yama: the God of Death

Yashoda: mother of Lord Krishna

Yavanas: Greeks, Romans

Yudhishthira: the eldest of the five Pandava brothers of the Mahabharatha

Glossary

aachaari: carpenter

aachamaram: country wood

Aagama: canon

Aakaasha Kannigai: celestial virgins

Aalwaar: Vaishnavite saint

aananda thaandava: Shiva's dance of creation in a mood of happiness

aarathi: circular motion made with a lamp or red lime water before the deity

aatta-karagam: the act of balancing flower-bedecked pots on the head during the folk dance *karagam*

Aavani: fifth month of the Tamil Calendar (August-September)

abhishekham: the sacred bath or anointing ceremony

addigai: stone-studded necklace

aduppu: stove

agartic: variety of muslin

ahal: small hand lamp

Aippasi: seventh month of the Tamil Calendar (October-November)

aksharaabhyaasa: ceremony at which the child begins his studies

alkul: cloth covering the hips and the loins

ambaari: the howdah or palanquin carried on top of an elephant

Amman: Mother Goddess

ammankovil : temple to the Mother Goddess

andaa: large copper boiler

angavastram: cloth worn by men to cover the upper torso

anna deepam: lamp surmounted by a mythical swan-like bird, the *hamsa* or *annapakshi*

annapakshi: mythical bird

anthivilaa: final appearance of the deity

apsaras: class of female divinities, sometimes called nymphs, inhabiting the sky, but often visiting the earth

arakku: dark red

aranaa kayar: hip-string

arasamaram: *pipal* tree

aruvaamanai: knife fastened to a plank for cutting vegetables

asili: stiff stone-set necklace

ashrafi: noble; in textiles, it is used to denote a coin design woven with golden thread, indicating noble or royal origin

ashtami: the eighth day after the new moon

asura: demon

avathaara: incarnation

azhingi: plant, the stem of which is used for weaving baskets

besari: jewel worn on the nose

bhakthi : faith or devotion

Bhogi-pandigai: festival of physical enjoyment celebrated in honour of Indra on the day preceding Pongal

bhootas: spirits

bindu: spot

bommai: doll

bommai kolu: arrangement of dolls during the festival of Navaraathri

bommalattam: puppetry

brahmothsavam: important annual festival celebrated in every temple

bullaakku: jewel hanging from the central membrane of the nose

Cancer: fourth sign of the zodiac represented by the crab

carbasina : cotton

chakra: sharp, circular missile, weapon of Lord Vishnu

chalabera: movable image

chalangai: bells

champa: fragrant yellow flower, the *Michelia champaca*

chandra pirai: percussion instrument made of thin parchment and shaped like a crescent

charkha: spinning wheel

chathurthi: the fourth day of the new moon

cheedai: savoury eatable made of rice flour and maida

cheeti: cotton material with small prints on a white or light background, origin of the English chintz

chellapetti: box to store betel leaves and areca nut

chik: screen made of palm leaf hung over the windows

Chithirai: first month of the Tamil Calendar (April-May)

Chithraa: constellation

Chithraa-Pournami: the full moon night in the month of Chithirai (April-May)

chokkaai: blouse

choli: blouse worn with the saree

chungidi: tie-dyed saree

chutti paanai: mud pot

cire perdue: 'lost wax', method of metal casting whereby a mould is formed around a wax model which is then melted away

dakshinaayanam: the sun's southerly course

dandu: palanquin or frame for carrying the deity on men's shoulders

darbha: a variety of grass, considered to be sacred

dashaavathaara: the ten incarnations of Vishnu

deepalakshmi: a lamp in the form of a woman holding a lamp, also known as paavai-vilakku

deepam: light or lamp

Deepavali: festival of lights occurring in the Tamil month of Aippasi (October-November)

deivam: deity

deva: celestial being

devadasi: temple dancer

dhoti: lower garment worn by men

dhvaja sthambha: flag post

dhyana: meditation

Dravida: the culture group to which the Tamil language belongs

dungari: coarse calico, origin of the English dungaree

durrie: rug

dvaarapaala: door-keeper

Dwaapara Yuga: the third yuga or age of the world consisting of 8,64,000 years

gajja golusu: heavy anklet

gajjaladdigai: heavy necklace made up of gold beads and either precious stones in the form of beads. or corals and black beads

gana: dwarf

gangaalam: large brass vessel to store water

ganjiraa: tambourine

garbhagriha: sanctum sanctorum

gettikkaappu: tight bracelet

ghatam: mud pot used as a percussion instrument

Gokulaashtami: birthday of Lord Krishna

golusu: anklet

gopi: yellow powder

gopuram: gateway to a South Indian temple

gottu vaadyam: string instrument, similar to the *veena* but without the frets

gowrikalam: wind instrument made of brass tubes fitted to each other

gundu: large beads flanking the *thaali*

guru: teacher

haasli: stiff stone-set necklace

hamsa: mythical bird

hamsa besari: swan-shaped stone-studded jewel worn on the nose

haveli: elaborately carved wooden houses, generally found in parts of Gujarat and Rajasthan

ikat: single weft or warp weave

izhuppu velai: etched gold with stone setting

jaali: net

jaalraa: percussion instrument used to keep time with devotional music

jaamdani: flowered muslin cloth

jadaguchchu: see *kunjalam*

jadanaagam: serpent-shaped long jewel, covering the hair braid

jaggery: coarse brown cane sugar

jallikattu: bull fight held during the Pongal festival

jamakaalam: carpet

jilpaabaavali: pendant worn on the hair above the ear and falling below the hair-line

jimikki: ear-drop (Hindi - *jhumka*)

kaal kaappu: protective anklet, generally worn by children

Kaamadhenu: mythical cow

Kaarthigai: eighth month of the Tamil calendar (November-December)

Kaarthigai deepam: Tamil festival of lights occurring in the month of Kaarthigai (November- December)

kaasumaalai: gold coin necklace

kaavadi: panel consisting of a pole and flowers or wooden carvings carried by devotees on the shoulders in fulfilment of a vow to Murugan

kaaval deivam: guardian deity

kadasal: lathe-turned lacquered wood

kadayam: armlet

kadira: country wood

kadukkan: single stone ear-stud

kalakam: mixture

kalam: pen

kalamkari: pen painting

kalanga: stain

kalasham: cornucopia

kalchutti: stone utensil

kammal: ear-studs

kandaangi selai: checked saree

Kandoori: Muslim festival held at Nagore in Tamilnadu

kanjam: musical instrument made of metal

kankanam: bangle

Kannan paadam: the feet of Lord Krishna

Kannimaar: virgin goddesses

kanti: stiff neck ornament, stiff necklace

karana: a Bharatanatyam pose

karagam: folk dance performed while balancing several flower-bedecked pots on the head; the pots balanced on the head during the folk dance

karandi: serving ladle

karpasa: cotton

karugamani: necklace

karungaali: ebony

kathribaavali: an ear ornament worn on the upper part of the outer ear

kautukabera: image taken around in procession

kavacham: metal covering

kempaddigai: ruby necklace

kempu manimaalai: necklace of rubies

kempu padakka muthumaalai: pearl necklace with a pendant of rubies

kirthimukha: grotesque face

kodi: rope or rope-like chain

kodi aduppu: double stove

kolam: ornamental design drawn with rice flour paste on the floor and walls

kolu: arrangement of dolls

kombu: musical instrument made of horn; a stick

koppu: ornament for the upper part of the ear

korai: variety of grass

kottadi: square room; checked design

kovil: temple

kozhambu: tamarind-based liquid dish

kudai: umbrella

kudam: pot

kudamuzhaa: two brass pots used as percussion instruments with the *panchamukhavaadyam*

kudirai: horse

kuluppai: grain container

kumbha: pot

kumkum: vermilion powder worn by Hindu women on their forehead

kundana: closed setting of precious stones

kunjalam: three decorated tassels worn at the ends of the three strands of a woman's hair braid

kunrimani: crab's eye seed

kuramaram: country wood

kurathi mani: gypsy beads

kuravan: gypsy

kuruthubaavali: ear ornament worn on the tragus of the ear

kuruvindam: cabochon rubies

kuthu-vilakku: standing lamp

kuyil-kan: cuckoo's eye

kuzhal: flute

linga: the phallic symbol of Lord Shiva

linga padakkam: pendant with *linga* or symbol of Lord Shiva

lolaakku: ornament hanging from the ear lobe

maadu: cattle

maadu salangai: chain of bells worn around the neck of cattle

maakal: soapstone

maangaamaalai: necklace of stone-studded golden mangoes

maangalya: married status

maattal: jewel joining the ear-stud to the hair

Maatu Pongal: the festival of cows, celebrated the day after Pongal

Madhuchchhista-vidhana: cire perdue or lost wax method of bronze casting

mahothsavam: annual festival

maida: tapioca flour

maiyi: black collyrium

makara: mythical crocodile; the tenth house of the zodiac

Makara yaazh: crocodile-shaped string instrument of ancient Tamilnadu

malai: hill

malaikulam: mat-weaving design of squares and geometrical shapes

mallimogi: jasmine buds

mandapa: pillared hall

mangalsuthra: talisman worn around the neck on a yellow string or gold chain as a sign of marriage, also known as the *thaali*

manjal: turmeric

manthram: sacred prayer

man-vilakku: mud lamp

mayil-kan: peacock's eye

mayil-kazhuthu: peacock-neck, as the colour peacock blue is known

medai: kitchen platform

melaakku: half-saree 2.5 metres long

metti: toe ring

modaka: sweet, considered to be the favourite of Lord Ganesha

mogappu: central jewel on the *oddiyaanam* or waistbelt

mohur: form of money used in the past

moodi koodai: woven basket covered with a lid

mookkupottu : nose ring

mookkuthi: nose jewel

moonru kaala pooja: worship performed in the temple in the morning , noon and evening

mooshika: mouse

moplapetu: Moplah or Muslim design

moram: winnowing pan

morsing: string instrument shaped like an elongated triangle and made of steel wire.

mridangam: percussion instrument made of leather thongs stretched tight over a long barrel-shaped body.

mudumakkal thazhi: burial urn

murukku: savoury eatable made of rice flour and black gram flour

muthu: gold ring studded with diamonds hanging from the nose; pearl

muthuchir: pearl-like beauty

muthukandi: pearl necklace

muzhavu-vaadya: percussion instrument

naadam: musical sound

naadaswaram: wind instrument played at marriages and temple festivals.

naadu-veedu : see *kolam*

naaga: snake

naagakal: snake stone

naagalinga: *linga* hooded by a snake

naagar: snake-shaped ornament worn on the head

naagavathu: an armlet fashioned as a snake coiled around the arm with a central cobra hood

naar pattu: cloth made of the fibre of trees, generally banana fibre, resembling silk

nagaas: design or pattern

nagaram: urban conglomeration, generally a town

nali: V-shaped ring presented to a bride at her wedding

Naraka Chathurdasi: another name for Deepavali

nathu: stone-studded nose ring

navami: the ninth day after the new moon

Navaraathri: the festival of nine days (*raathri* means night)

navarathna: the nine sacred gems

nayanonmilan: the sacred rite to communicate sight to an idol

nebula venti : literally "woven wind"; name of a textile

nellikkaai manimaalai: gooseberry-bead necklace

nellu: paddy

nithyothsavam: daily festival

oddiyaanam: waist-belt

oosivaanam: 'needle' lines (literally 'needle sky') woven into silk sarees as thin horizontal lines of gold, giving the cloth a shimmering effect

paaimadi: folded or pleated

paalayankottai : used to describe a variety of checked saree

paambadam: heavy ear ornament which drags the lobe down to form a large hole

paan: roll of betel leaf and areca nuts for chewing

paatil: bracelet

paavaadai: ankle-length skirt worn by young girls

paavai-vilakku: see *deepalakshmi*

padi: step

padi kolam: ornamental square or rectangular designs, symbolic of steps around a courtyard, drawn with rice flour paste or powder on the floor

padma: lotus

palaa: jackwood

pallu: the end of a woman's saree or a man's upper cloth (*angavastram*)

pampaadi: a musical instrument

pancha kritya: five religious activities

panchaloha: the five metals, i.e. gold, silver,copper, tin and lead

panchamukhavaadyam: five-faced percussion instrument

panchapaathra: cup used for keeping water at religious ceremonies

pancharangi: five colours

Panguni: twelfth month of the Tamil Calendar (March-April)

Panguni Uthiram: the constellation *thiram* in the month of Panguni (March-April), celebrated as a festival

panirchombu: rose water pot

papli: the papaya fruit

pariyakam: *navarathna* bangles

pattaabhishekam: coronation

pattu: silk (formerly, fold)

peeli: toe ring

pipal: *Ficus religiosa* (bo tree)

Pongal: the harvest festival of Tamilnadu, coinciding with the sun's entry into Capricorn in mid-January

pongal: a dish made of rice and split green gram

pooja: worship

poojaari: priest

poonal: the sacred thread worn by Brahmins and upper caste Hindus

poornakumbha: pot containing water, mango leaves and a coconut, symbolic of sanctity and plenty, generally used in temple rituals; cornucopia

poykaal kudirai: dummy-legged horse, a popular folk dance

praakaara: circumambulatory passage

prabha: circle of light

prabhaamandala: halo of fire

Puduchcheri golusu: a kind of silver anklet

pulinagam: tiger claw

Puraanas: ancient legends of the Hindus

Purattaasi: sixth month of the Tamil Calendar (September-October)

pushpapalaka: an open shrine

Pushya: a constellation

raajyaabhishekham: coronation

raakkodi, raakkadi: circular ornament worn on the head

raakshasa: demon

raathri: night

rakshai: amulet

rakta chandana: red sandalwood

Ramapattaabhishekam : Rama's coronation

ratha, ratham: chariot; small pillared shrine

rathna kanti: jewel-studded stiff necklace

rekha: patch

rishi: sage

R'ta: the cosmic order as propounded in the Vedas

rudraaksham: *Elaeocarpus ganitrus* or its berry, strung into a rosary; *rudraaksham* design means sovereign design

saaligraamam: a species of ammonite revered as a representation of Vishnu

saambaar: liquid accompaniment to rice made of tamarind, lentils, spices and vegetables

saatai: whip

sabha: hall

sadaari: crown-shaped metal cone mounted with feet representing those of Lord Rama

salangai: metal bells worn on the ankles by dancers and children, or around the neck of cows; gold beads strung into a necklace and interspersed with black or coral beads

samaashrayanam mudrai: tattoos

sangam: meeting, a literary reference to ancient conferences

sangu: conch

sanyaasi: ascetic

sappaangu kattai: Brazil wood

Saptha Kannigai: the seven holy virgins

Saptha Maatrika: the seven divine mothers

sapthaswara: the seven musical notes

saree: long piece of cotton or silk fabric worn by Indian women and draped over the shoulder

sengaali: rosewood

seppu thirumeni: metal image(generally of greater copper content)

Shaastras: scriptures, written works or canons of science, philosophy, arts, etc

shankha: conch

shembaga poo: the champa flower

shevarikottai: hair ornament

shikhara: see *vimaana*

shilpi: sculptor

shiraschakra: literally translated as 'head wheel',it signifies the halo at the back of the head of a figure.

shloka: hymn of praise

shodashopachaaram: the sixteen acts of worship or ritual paid to the temple deity

shombu: pot

shruthi: musical tone

shungudi: tie-dyed saree made in Madurai

sinam: silk

singam: lion

sisal: screw pine

siththu: stay ring to hold the *metti* in place

spatika linga: crystal *linga*

sthapathi: architect, master craftsman or sculptor

sthirabera: immovable image

sthree-dhana: the property given to a girl at her wedding.

sudai: stucco

surya pirai: percussion instrument made of thin parchment and circular like the sun; jewel worn on the head

swara: musical note

swarasthaanam: the position of the musical notes

thaala: measure of height, generally a span measured by the thumb and middle finger

thaali: talisman worn around the neck on a yellow string or gold chain as a sign of marriage, also known as *mangalsuthra*

thaandava: dance, especially the dance of Shiva

thaatankam: ear ornament

thaazham : screw pine

thaazhambu: screw pine flower

thachar: carpenter

Thai: tenth month of the Tamil Calendar (January-February)

Thai Poosam: the day when the constellation Pushya appears in the month of Thai (January-February)

thalaisaamaan: jewellery worn on the head

thamakku: tom-tom (a drum)

thamburaa: string instrument used to indicate the *shruthi*

thandai: stiff anklet

thandora: percussion instrument; practice of beating the drums.

thapatai: a small drum or tabouret

tharavaad: traditional wooden house of Kerala; ancestral house

thavalai: metal vessel

thavil: percussion instrument played by beating the sides with sticks

ther: wooden chariot used to carry the deity during festivals

thilakam: elongated mark worn on the forehead

thinnai: raised floor or veranda either outside or inside the house

thirugu poo: a circular hair ornament with a spiral spring which is screwed into the braid

thirugusaamanthi poo: crysanthemum-shaped hair ornament with a spiral spring which is screwed into the braid

thiruvizhaa: festival

thoda: stone-set bracelet

thodu: earring

thombai: cylindrical cloth ornament hung around a temple car (*ther* or *ratha*)

thombu: red dye

thoon: pillar

thoranam: cord of mango leaves or cloth hung over a doorway

thulasi: basil plant (*Ocimum sanctum*), which has a religious significance for Hindus

thulasi maadam: square construction enclosing the *thulasi* plant

uchchippooteeka: jewel worn on the hair by children

uddharani: spoon used with the *panchapaathra* at religious ceremonies

udukkai: small drum shaped like an hour-glass generally associated with Shiva

udumbu: iguana

ulakkai: pestle

ulukkai: small percussion insturment, similar to that held by Nataraja

ural: mortar

uruli: flat wide-mouthed vessel

urumi: percussion instrument played with a curved stick, which makes the sound of a tiger roaring

Utharaayanam: the sun's entry into Capricorn in mid-January

Uthiram: One of the 27 asterisms

uthiri poo: loose flowers

uthrasam: see *rudraaksham*

uthsavam: festival

uthsavamurthi: image used at festivals

vaahana: vehicle

vaazhai poo: banana flower

vaidoorya: the chrysoberyl, a yellowish-green gem

Vaikaasi: second month of the Tamil Calendar (May-June)

vaira: diamond

vaira addigai: diamond necklace

valai: bangle

vangiya vaadya: flute

vangiyam: flute

vanki: armlet

Varalakshmi vratham: worship of goddess Lakshmi by women for conferring on them health, wealth and maangalya

Vasantha Navaraathri: spring festival

veena: string instrument

veeran: hero

vel: lance

veldhaari: wavy horizontal lines woven into the saree

vempal: neem wood

verati: dried cow-dung, generally used as fuel

veshti: lower garment worn by men

vetrilaipaakku petti: box for betel leaves and areca nut

vibhoothi: sacred ash worn on the forehead by the followers of Devi, Shiva and the Shaivite deities

Vijaya-dashami: the tenth day of Navaraathri

villadi vaadyam: folk instrument in the shape of a bow

vimaana: the central spire of a temple; flying chariot

Vinayaka Chathurthi: festival in Aavani (August-September) in honour of Lord Ganesha, when clay idols of Ganesha are made and worshipped

vismaya mudra: hand movement denoting surprise

vratham: vow

vriksha-deepam: tree-like lamp

vriksha devatha: spirit of the tree

vrishabham: bull

yaali: mythical lion

yaazh: ancient string instrument, no longer in use

yagna: oblation or sacrifice

yajamaana: householder

Yakshi: female spirit

Yoga: Indian system of philosophic meditation and exercise, aiming for salvation

yuga: epoch

zamindar: landlord

zari: gold thread

Bibliography

Abraham, T.M. *Handicrafts in India*. New Delhi, Mathew Cherian Graphics, Columbia, 1964.

Appasamy, Jaya. *Indian Paintings on Glass*. New Delhi, Indian Council for Cultural Relations, 1980.

Appasamy, Jaya. *Tanjavur paintings of the Maratha period*. New Delhi, Abhinav Publications, 1980.

Brijbhusan, Jamila. *Masterpieces of Indian Jewellery*. Bombay, D.B. Taraporevala Sons & Co. Private Ltd., 1979.

Dhamija, Jasleen. *Indian arts and crafts*. New Delhi, National Book Trust, 1977.

Dikshitar, Ramachandra. *Silappadikaaram*, tr. by Humphrey Milford. London, Oxford University Press, 1939.

Harinarayana, N. ``Tanjore Painting on Glass'' *Nunkalai* Vol. 1.No.1. Dec. 1981.

Inglis, Stephen. *A Village Art of South India*. Madurai. Kamaraj University.

Jagadisa Ayyar, P.V. *South Indian Festivities*. Madras, Higginbothams Limited,1921.

Kanakasabhai V. *The Tamils Eighteen Hundred Years Ago*. New Delhi, Asian Educational Services, 1979.

Kandaswamy S. "Terracotta figures", *Nunkalai,* vol.2; No. 2, July-Dec. 1983.

Krishnaswamy, S. *Musical Instruments of India*. New Delhi, Ministry of Information and Broadcasting, 1971.

Mehta, R.J. *The Handicrafts and Industrial Arts of India*. Bombay, D.B. Taraporevala Sons & Co. Pvt. Ltd., 1960.

Nagaswamy R. *Masterpieces of Early South Indian Bronzes*. New Delhi, National Museum, 1983.

Nilakanta Sastri, K.A. *A History of South India*. Bombay, Oxford University Press, 1971.

Pal, M.K.*Crafts & Craftsmen in Traditional India*. New Delhi, Kanak Publications, 1978.

Rosenthal, Ethel. *The Story of Indian Music and Its Instruments*. New Delhi, Oriental Books Reprint Corporation, 1980.

Sambamoorthy, P. *Catalogue of Musical Instruments Exhibited in the Government Museum*. Madras, 1976.

Seethalai Sathanar. *Manimekhalai*. Madras, Saiva Siddhanta Publishers & Co., 1955.

Sivaramamurti, C. *The Art of India*. New York, Harry N. Abrams Inc., 1977.

Sivaramamurti, C. *Five Thousand Years of the Art of India*. New York, Harry N. Abrams Inc., Reprinted 1977.

Sivaramamurti C. *South Indian Bronzes*. New Delhi, Lalit Kala Akademi, 1981.

Slater, C. *The Dravidian Element in Indian Culture*. London, Ernest Benn Ltd., 1924.

South Zone Cultural Centre. *Spell of the South*. Madras, 1987.

Splendours of Tamilnadu. Bombay, *Marg* Publication, 1980.

Swaminatha Iyer, U.V. *Pathu Pattu Mulam Nachinar Kiniyar Urai*. Madras, Kabir Publishers , 1950.

Swarup, Shanti, *5000 years of Arts & Crafts in India Pakistan*, Bombay, D.B. Taraporevala & Co. 1968.

Thurston, E. *Castes & Tribes of Southern India*. New Delhi, Cosmo Publications, 1924.

Biographical Notes :

M. REDDAPPA NAIDU is the Deputy Director of the Weavers' Service Centre, Madras. He has specialised in South Indian textiles, particularly block printing and weaving. A well-known artist, Naidu has held several one-man shows in India and abroad, and has received several awards.

V.N. SRINIVASA DESIKAN has a PhD in Ancient History and is the Curator for Arts and Archaeology in the Government Museum, Madras. He has participated in several explorations and excavations, conducted surveys of antiquities and discovered several prehistoric and historic sites and temples. Author of several papers in leading journals and several books on South Indian art, he has specialised in the identification of South Indian antiquities, especially bronzes, and in the dating of South Indian sculptures in all media.

SHAKUNTHALA JAGANNATHAN holds an MA (Hons) in Economics from Madras University and an MA from Columbia University. She worked in the Department of Tourism, Government of India, from 1955 to 1985 and retired as the Regional Director in Bombay. In the course of her career she introduced several dynamic new ideas to increase tourism to India. She has also written several articles on Indian women, culture and tourism and is the author of two best-selling books, *Hinduism* and *India* and *Plan Your Own Holiday*. She is currently working on a book on Indian jewellery.

DEBORAH DEAL THIAGARAJAN has an MA from the University of Pennsylvania and is currently doing her PhD in Archaeology and Ancient Indian Culture from the University of Madras. She is the Convenor for the Indian National Trust for Art and Cultural Heritage (INTACH) in Madras and has specialised in the study of Chettinad wood carvings.

T. LOGANATHA SHARMA is the Director of the Centre for Musical Instruments set up by the office of the Development Commissioner for Handicrafts, Govt. of India. He has a PhD in Musicology. He has written several articles on the subject as well as a book on musical instruments. He has also developed some musical instruments such as a portable *thamburaa* to be used by travelling musicians.

GANAPATHI STHAPATHI belongs to a traditional family of *sthapathis* from the days of Rajaraja Chola. His ancestors were descendants of the great sculptors of the tenth century Brihadeeshvara Temple at Thanjavur. A Sanskrit scholar he has studied traditional architecture and sculpture from his father and uncle and has designed and executed several temples and sculptures in India and abroad. He is a holder of several awards and titles such as Silpakala Rathnam, Silpa Kalanidhi, Silpakala Chakravarthi and Silpa Samrat. He has published a book on iconometry and is currently preparing two books on iconography and architecture. He has been the Head of the Government College of Architecture and Sculpture in Mamallapuram for the last 26 years.

SASHIKALA is an architect and a student of Ganapathi Sthapathi.

MEENA MUTHIAH, the Kumara Rani of Chettinad, studied the Thanjavur (Tanjore) school of painting from traditional craftsmen and set up the Kumararaja Muthiah School of Traditional Arts and Crafts at Chettinad House in Madras. The school trains craftsmen in Thanjavur paintings, bronze casting and weaving. She has exhibited her own Thanjavur paintings in New York, Bombay, Madras, and Bangalore. Muthiah is also an educationist and social worker.

P.SAVARI RAJU is the Cottage Industries Manager in the District Industries Centre at Thiruchirapalli. For several years he worked in various capacities in the Tamilnadu Handicrafts Development Corporation (Poompuhar) in the production and sales of handicrafts, for which he started training centres all over Tamilnadu. He has held exhibitions of Tamilnadu handicrafts at various centres in India.

SREELATHA VASUDEVAN has an MA in Ancient History and Archaeology from the University of Madras and is currently doing her PhD from the University of Delhi. She was the Programme Officer at the C.P. Ramaswami Aiyar Institute of Indological Research. Her thesis is on the forms of Durga in Tamilnadu.

GITA RAM is the Honorary Secretary of the Madras chapter of the Crafts Council of India. Her interest in the crafts has led her to study and collect a variety of crafts, particularly folk crafts and dynamic toys.

K.E. SUPRIYA was a research scholar at the C.P. Ramaswami Aiyar Institute of Indological Research. After doing her MA in Fine Arts, she joined the Institute to conduct a study of folk toys of South India, in connection with which she has visited all the major toy-making sites and collected data about the craft and craftsmen.

Captions

Endpaper

Kanchipuram shot-silk saree, detail

A gold brocade border of a silk saree, made up of floral designs and mythical birds. The *zari* is woven with silk threads coated with silver and polished with gold.

Page 4-5

Metal nut-cracker

(Courtesy : Madras Museum).

Page 1

Ganesha

Dancing Ganesha, a form that has become very popular in recent years. The craftsman's ingenuity is great, considering the co-ordination of the stunted, pot-bellied figure in a dancing pose. This is a contemporary bronze.

(Courtesy : Poompuhar)

Page 7

Stylised metal elephant, detail

The art of metal casting and finishing reached great heights in Tamilnadu. The same popular motifs were used in various crafts. This metal elephant, for example, is repeated on the stone walls of the Aavadaiyar Temple near Karaikudi, on the wooden printing blocks of Pudukottai, on the prints on cotton saris and on the zari woven into the silks.

Page 2-3

Bronze Nataraja, Chola period